The Art of Positive Thinking

Self-help, Volume 4

Timothy Scott Phillips

Published by Arcane Horizons Publishing, 2024.

THE ART OF POSITIVE THINKING

First edition. November 28, 2024.

ISBN: 979-8227741813

Written by Timothy Scott Phillips.

Table of Contents

To all who seek the light even in the darkest moments,This book is for the dreamers, the believers, and the resilient soulswho refuse to let life's challenges dim their optimism.

May your journey toward positivity bring you strength, joy, and endless possibilities.

Chapter 1: Understanding Positive Thinking

Definition and Importance of Positive Thinking

Positive thinking, at its core, involves a mental and emotional attitude that focuses on the bright side of life and expects positive outcomes. It's the practice of focusing on the good in any given situation and maintaining an optimistic outlook. Positive thinking doesn't mean ignoring the reality of life's challenges; instead, it means approaching those challenges with a constructive and proactive mindset.

Key Elements of Positive Thinking

1. OPTIMISM: THE TENDENCY to expect the best possible outcome or dwell on the most hopeful aspects of a situation.

2. Resilience: The ability to recover quickly from setbacks and remain optimistic despite adversity.

3. Gratitude: Appreciating what you have rather than focusing on what you lack.

4. Mindfulness: Staying present in the moment and fully engaging with your current experiences.

The Importance of Positive Thinking

POSITIVE THINKING IS more than just a feel-good exercise. It has profound implications for your mental, emotional, and physical well-being.

Mental Health Benefits:

- **REDUCED STRESS**: Positive thinking helps manage stress by reducing the impact of negative thinking and anxiety.

- **Enhanced Mood**: Positive thinkers tend to experience higher levels of joy, satisfaction, and overall happiness.

Emotional Benefits:

- INCREASED RESILIENCE: A positive outlook helps individuals bounce back from setbacks more effectively.

- Improved Relationships: Positivity fosters better communication, empathy, and trust, strengthening personal and professional relationships.

Physical Health Benefits:

- LOWER RISK OF CARDIOVASCULAR Disease: Studies have shown that optimists are less likely to suffer from heart disease.

- Stronger Immune System: A positive mindset can enhance immune function, making the body more resistant to illnesses.

Career and Financial Success:

- ENHANCED PRODUCTIVITY: Positive thinking boosts creativity and problem-solving skills, leading to better performance at work.

- Career Advancement: Optimists are more likely to pursue opportunities and persevere through challenges, leading to greater career success.

Historical Perspectives on Optimism

THE CONCEPT OF POSITIVE thinking and optimism has roots that trace back to ancient philosophies and religious teachings. Throughout history, various cultures and thought leaders have recognized the power of a positive mindset.

Ancient Philosophies

STOICISM:

- The Stoics, ancient Greek philosophers, believed in the importance of focusing on what can be controlled and accepting what cannot. They emphasized the power of perception and maintaining a rational and positive outlook regardless of external circumstances.

Buddhism:

- Buddhism teaches the principle of mindfulness and living in the present moment. It emphasizes the importance of positive thoughts, compassion, and gratitude in achieving a state of inner peace and enlightenment.

Confucianism:

- Confucianism, a philosophy rooted in Chinese culture, advocates for the cultivation of virtue, moral integrity, and positive human relationships. It encourages individuals to focus on self-improvement and the betterment of society.

Religious Teachings

CHRISTIANITY:

- Christianity promotes the virtues of faith, hope, and love. The teachings of Jesus Christ emphasize the importance of a positive and forgiving attitude, as well as the power of faith and hope in overcoming life's challenges.

Islam:

- Islam teaches the importance of patience (sabr) and gratitude (shukr). Believers are encouraged to maintain a positive attitude and trust in God's plan, even during difficult times.

Hinduism:

- Hinduism emphasizes the law of karma, which suggests that positive actions and thoughts lead to positive outcomes. The practice of yoga and meditation in Hinduism also fosters a positive and balanced state of mind.

Modern Developments

The New Thought Movement:

- THE NEW THOUGHT MOVEMENT emerged in the 19th century, emphasizing the power of positive thinking and mental healing. Prominent figures like Ralph Waldo Emerson and William James contributed to this philosophy, advocating for the idea that thoughts can shape reality.

Positive Psychology:

- IN THE LATE 20TH CENTURY, positive psychology emerged as a scientific field dedicated to studying human happiness and well-being. Researchers like Martin Seligman and Mihaly Csikszentmihalyi explored the benefits of optimism, gratitude, and other positive traits, providing a robust scientific foundation for positive thinking.

Scientific Evidence Supporting Positive Thinking

POSITIVE THINKING HAS been extensively studied within the fields of psychology, medicine, and neuroscience. The evidence supporting its benefits is both compelling and multifaceted.

Psychological Studies

Optimism and Well-Being:

- A LANDMARK STUDY BY psychologists Charles S. Carver and Michael F. Scheier in the 1980s demonstrated that optimists tend to experience better mental health, greater life satisfaction, and reduced levels of depression and anxiety compared to pessimists.

Cognitive-Behavioral Therapy (CBT):

- CBT IS A WIDELY-USED therapeutic approach that focuses on changing negative thought patterns to improve mental health. Numerous studies have shown that CBT, which incorporates principles of positive thinking, is effective in treating depression, anxiety disorders, and other mental health conditions.

Medical Studies

Cardiovascular Health:

- RESEARCH PUBLISHED in the journal "Circulation" found that individuals with a positive outlook had a significantly lower risk of developing cardiovascular disease. Optimists were found to have better heart health, lower blood pressure, and reduced mortality rates from heart-related issues.

Immune Function:

- A STUDY CONDUCTED by the University of Kentucky showed that positive emotions and optimism can boost the immune system. Participants with a positive outlook exhibited stronger immune responses, indicating a greater ability to fight off infections.

Longevity:

- The "Nun Study," a longitudinal research project, found that nuns who expressed more positive emotions in their early writings lived significantly longer than those who expressed fewer positive emotions. This study highlighted the link between positive thinking and increased lifespan.

Neuroscientific Research

Brain Plasticity:

- NEUROSCIENTIFIC RESEARCH has shown that positive thinking can lead to changes in brain structure and function. Neuroplasticity, the brain's ability to reorganize itself, allows positive thoughts and experiences to strengthen neural connections associated with happiness and well-being.

Stress Reduction:

- STUDIES USING FUNCTIONAL magnetic resonance imaging (fMRI) have demonstrated that practicing positive thinking techniques, such as mindfulness and gratitude, can reduce activity in the brain's stress-related regions, leading to lower levels of cortisol, the stress hormone.

Conclusion

Positive thinking is a powerful tool that can transform your life in profound ways. Its benefits are supported by historical wisdom, religious teachings, and a growing body of scientific evidence. By understanding the importance of positive thinking and incorporating its principles into your daily life, you can enhance your mental, emotional, and physical well-being, build stronger relationships, and achieve greater success in your personal and professional endeavors.

As you embark on this journey to cultivate a positive mindset, remember that it is a practice that requires commitment and consistency. With time and effort, you can develop the habit of positive thinking and experience the transformative power of optimism in every aspect of your life.

Chapter 2: The Benefits of Positive Thinking

Positive thinking, often dismissed as mere optimism, is a transformative approach to life that can lead to significant improvements in various aspects of well-being. It involves adopting a mindset that focuses on the good in any situation, fosters resilience, and promotes a healthier, happier, and more fulfilling life. In this chapter, we delve deep into the numerous benefits of positive thinking, exploring its impact on mental health, physical health, relationships, and career success.

Mental Health Benefits

MENTAL HEALTH IS A critical component of overall well-being, influencing how we think, feel, and act. Positive thinking plays a crucial role in enhancing mental health by reducing stress, anxiety, and depression, and promoting a more balanced and resilient mindset.

Reduced Stress

STRESS IS AN INEVITABLE part of life, but how we manage it can significantly impact our mental health. Positive thinking helps mitigate the effects of stress by promoting a more optimistic outlook on life's challenges.

- Cognitive Reframing: One of the key techniques in positive thinking is cognitive reframing, which involves altering how we perceive stressful situations. Instead of viewing a challenge as an insurmountable obstacle, positive thinkers see it as an opportunity for growth and learning. This shift in perspective reduces the psychological burden of stress and fosters a more proactive approach to problem-solving.

- Mindfulness and Relaxation: Positive thinking encourages practices such as mindfulness and relaxation techniques, which are effective in reducing stress. Mindfulness involves staying present and fully engaged in the moment, reducing the tendency to ruminate on past failures or future anxieties.

Relaxation techniques, such as deep breathing and meditation, help calm the mind and alleviate stress.

Enhanced Mood and Emotional Resilience

POSITIVE THINKING SIGNIFICANTLY impacts mood and emotional resilience, leading to a more balanced and stable emotional state.

- Increased Serotonin Levels: Positive thoughts and emotions have been linked to increased levels of serotonin, a neurotransmitter that plays a crucial role in regulating mood. Higher serotonin levels are associated with feelings of happiness and well-being.

- Greater Emotional Resilience: Positive thinkers tend to be more resilient in the face of adversity. They have a better capacity to bounce back from setbacks and maintain emotional stability during difficult times. This resilience stems from their ability to see the silver lining in challenging situations and maintain hope for the future.

Reduced Anxiety and Depression

ANXIETY AND DEPRESSION are common mental health disorders that can be alleviated through the practice of positive thinking.

- Cognitive Behavioral Therapy (CBT): CBT is a therapeutic approach that incorporates positive thinking to treat anxiety and depression. It involves identifying and challenging negative thought patterns and replacing them with more positive and realistic ones. Studies have shown that CBT is highly effective in reducing symptoms of anxiety and depression.

- Gratitude Practice: Practicing gratitude is a powerful tool in combating anxiety and depression. By focusing on what we are grateful for, we shift our attention away from negative thoughts and foster a sense of appreciation and contentment. Research has shown that individuals who regularly practice gratitude experience lower levels of anxiety and depression.

Physical Health Improvements

THE BENEFITS OF POSITIVE thinking extend beyond mental health, significantly impacting physical health as well. A positive mindset can lead to better health outcomes, increased longevity, and an overall improved quality of life.

Improved Cardiovascular Health

POSITIVE THINKING HAS been linked to better cardiovascular health, reducing the risk of heart disease and related conditions.

- Lower Blood Pressure: Optimistic individuals tend to have lower blood pressure, which reduces the strain on the heart and decreases the risk of heart disease. This is partly due to the stress-reducing effects of positive thinking, as chronic stress is a known risk factor for hypertension.

- Reduced Risk of Heart Disease: A study published in the journal "Circulation" found that individuals with a positive outlook had a significantly lower risk of developing cardiovascular disease. Optimists were found to have better heart health and reduced mortality rates from heart-related issues.

Enhanced Immune Function

A POSITIVE MINDSET can boost the immune system, making the body more resistant to illnesses and infections.

- Stronger Immune Response: Research conducted by the University of Kentucky showed that positive emotions and optimism can enhance immune function. Participants with a positive outlook exhibited stronger immune responses, indicating a greater ability to fight off infections.

- Reduced Inflammation: Chronic inflammation is associated with various health conditions, including autoimmune diseases and cancer. Positive thinking has been linked to lower levels of inflammation, reducing the risk of these conditions. This is believed to be due to the stress-reducing and immune-boosting effects of a positive mindset.

Increased Longevity

POSITIVE THINKING HAS been associated with increased longevity, allowing individuals to live longer, healthier lives.

- The Nun Study: The "Nun Study," a longitudinal research project, found that nuns who expressed more positive emotions in their early writings lived significantly longer than those who expressed fewer positive emotions. This study highlighted the link between positive thinking and increased lifespan.

- Telomere Length: Telomeres are protective caps at the ends of chromosomes that shorten with age. Shorter telomeres are associated with aging and increased risk of age-related diseases. Research has shown that individuals with a positive outlook tend to have longer telomeres, indicating a slower rate of aging and a reduced risk of age-related diseases.

Better Pain Management

POSITIVE THINKING CAN also play a role in pain management, reducing the perception of pain and improving overall well-being.

- Pain Perception: Studies have shown that individuals with a positive outlook tend to perceive pain as less intense compared to those with a negative mindset. This is partly due to the stress-reducing and mood-enhancing effects of positive thinking, which can alter the brain's perception of pain.

- Coping Strategies: Positive thinkers are more likely to use effective coping strategies to manage pain, such as relaxation techniques, physical activity, and seeking social support. These strategies help reduce the impact of pain on daily life and improve overall well-being.

Enhancing Relationships and Social Interactions

POSITIVE THINKING PLAYS a crucial role in building and maintaining healthy relationships and enhancing social interactions. It fosters empathy, improves communication, and strengthens social bonds.

Improved Communication

EFFECTIVE COMMUNICATION is the cornerstone of healthy relationships, and positive thinking can enhance communication skills.

- Active Listening: Positive thinkers are more likely to engage in active listening, which involves fully focusing on the speaker, understanding their message, and responding thoughtfully. Active listening fosters empathy and trust, strengthening relationships.

- Constructive Feedback: Positive thinkers provide constructive feedback, focusing on solutions and growth rather than criticism. This approach fosters a supportive and collaborative environment, enhancing relationship satisfaction.

Enhanced Empathy and Compassion

EMPATHY AND COMPASSION are essential for building strong, healthy relationships, and positive thinking promotes these qualities.

- Empathy: Positive thinkers are more attuned to the emotions and experiences of others, making them more empathetic. Empathy allows individuals to understand and connect with others on a deeper level, fostering stronger relationships.

- Compassion: Positive thinking fosters compassion, which involves recognizing the suffering of others and taking action to alleviate it. Compassion strengthens social bonds and promotes a sense of community and belonging.

Strengthened Social Bonds

POSITIVE THINKING ENHANCES social interactions and strengthens social bonds, leading to more fulfilling relationships.

- Social Support: Positive thinkers are more likely to seek and provide social support, which is crucial for maintaining healthy relationships. Social support enhances well-being and resilience, helping individuals cope with life's challenges.

- Positive Social Interactions: Positive thinking fosters positive social interactions, characterized by kindness, respect, and mutual support. These interactions strengthen social bonds and promote a sense of connection and belonging.

Conflict Resolution

POSITIVE THINKING PLAYS a crucial role in conflict resolution, promoting peaceful and constructive solutions to disagreements.

- Constructive Approach: Positive thinkers approach conflicts with a constructive mindset, focusing on finding solutions rather than dwelling on problems. This approach fosters collaboration and mutual understanding, leading to more effective conflict resolution.

- Emotional Regulation: Positive thinking enhances emotional regulation, allowing individuals to manage their emotions during conflicts. This promotes calm and rational discussions, reducing the likelihood of escalation and fostering peaceful resolutions.

Career and Financial Success

POSITIVE THINKING CAN significantly impact career and financial success, enhancing productivity, creativity, and resilience in the workplace.

Enhanced Productivity and Performance

POSITIVE THINKING BOOSTS productivity and performance, leading to greater career success.

- Motivation and Engagement: Positive thinkers are more motivated and engaged in their work, leading to higher levels of productivity. They approach tasks with enthusiasm and a can-do attitude, fostering a more productive work environment.

- Problem-Solving Skills: Positive thinking enhances problem-solving skills, promoting creativity and innovation. Positive thinkers are more likely to approach challenges with an open mind and find effective solutions.

Career Advancement

POSITIVE THINKING PLAYS a crucial role in career advancement, promoting perseverance, adaptability, and leadership skills.

- Perseverance: Positive thinkers are more likely to persevere through challenges and setbacks, demonstrating resilience and determination. This perseverance is crucial for career advancement and achieving long-term goals.

- Adaptability: Positive thinking fosters adaptability, allowing individuals to navigate changes and uncertainties in the workplace. Adaptable individuals are more likely to thrive in dynamic work environments and seize new opportunities.

- Leadership Skills: Positive thinkers are more likely to exhibit leadership qualities, such as empathy, effective communication, and problem-solving skills. These qualities enhance their ability to lead and inspire others, promoting career advancement.

Financial Success

POSITIVE THINKING CAN also impact financial success, promoting prudent financial decisions and resilience in the face of financial challenges.

- Prudent Financial Decisions: Positive thinkers are more likely to make prudent financial decisions, focusing on long-term goals and avoiding impulsive spending. They approach financial challenges with a constructive mindset, seeking solutions and opportunities for growth.

- Resilience in Financial Challenges: Positive thinking enhances resilience in the face of financial challenges, promoting a proactive and solutions-oriented approach. Positive thinkers are more likely to seek support and resources, navigate financial difficulties, and achieve financial stability.

Conclusion

Positive thinking is a powerful tool that can transform various aspects of life, from mental and physical health to relationships and career success. By adopting a positive mindset, individuals can experience reduced stress, enhanced emotional resilience, improved physical health, stronger relationships, and greater career and financial success. The benefits of positive thinking are supported by a growing body of scientific evidence, highlighting its profound impact on overall well-being. Embracing positive thinking is a journey that requires commitment and practice, but the rewards are well worth the effort. By cultivating a positive mindset, individuals can unlock their full potential and lead a healthier, happier, and more fulfilling life.

Chapter 3: The Mindset of Optimism

Fixed vs. Growth Mindset

The concept of mindset, particularly fixed and growth mindsets, was popularized by Carol Dweck, a renowned psychologist from Stanford University. Dweck's groundbreaking research delineated how our beliefs about our abilities and intelligence can significantly impact our success and happiness. Understanding these mindsets and how to cultivate a growth mindset is fundamental to fostering optimism.

Fixed Mindset

A FIXED MINDSET IS characterized by the belief that our abilities, intelligence, and talents are static traits. People with a fixed mindset believe that they are born with a certain level of intelligence and talent, and that these attributes cannot be significantly changed. This belief leads to a desire to appear intelligent and competent at all times, and often results in avoiding challenges and giving up easily when faced with obstacles.

For example, a student with a fixed mindset might think, "I'm just not good at math," and thus avoid math classes or studying, believing that no amount of effort will change their innate ability. Similarly, an employee might shy away from taking on new projects or learning new skills, fearing failure and judgment.

The fixed mindset also tends to foster a deterministic view of the world. Success and failure are seen as reflections of inherent worth, rather than outcomes influenced by effort, strategy, and learning. This mindset can lead to a fear of failure, a reluctance to take risks, and an overall pessimistic outlook on one's ability to grow and improve.

Growth Mindset

IN CONTRAST, A GROWTH mindset is based on the belief that abilities and intelligence can be developed through dedication, hard work, and perseverance. People with a growth mindset see challenges as opportunities to learn and grow, and they view failure as a natural part of the learning process.

A student with a growth mindset might think, "I can improve my math skills with practice and effort," and therefore seek out additional help, study more diligently, and embrace difficult problems as chances to learn. An employee with a growth mindset might take on challenging projects and seek out new skills, understanding that these experiences will contribute to their personal and professional development.

The growth mindset fosters a love for learning and a resilience that is essential for great accomplishment. This mindset leads to a more optimistic and proactive approach to life's challenges. Instead of feeling threatened by failure, individuals with a growth mindset see it as a stepping stone to success. They believe that effort and persistence can lead to improvement and achievement, and this belief propels them to keep trying, even when faced with setbacks.

Developing a Positive Attitude

A POSITIVE ATTITUDE is an essential component of an optimistic mindset. It not only influences our behavior and decisions but also affects our overall well-being. Developing a positive attitude involves cultivating habits and perspectives that enhance our ability to see the good in situations, stay hopeful, and remain resilient in the face of adversity.

The Power of Positive Thinking

POSITIVE THINKING IS not about ignoring reality or sugar-coating difficulties. Rather, it is about focusing on solutions, seeing challenges as opportunities, and maintaining a hopeful outlook. Research has shown that positive thinking can improve physical health, reduce stress, and enhance overall life satisfaction.

One way to develop positive thinking is through the practice of gratitude. Taking time each day to reflect on what you are grateful for can shift your focus from what is lacking to what is abundant in your life. This simple practice can help rewire your brain to recognize and appreciate the positive aspects of your life.

Another technique is to reframe negative thoughts. When faced with a challenging situation, instead of dwelling on what could go wrong, try to identify potential benefits or learning opportunities. For example, if you are worried about a difficult project at work, consider how this project could help you develop new skills or advance your career.

The Role of Self-Talk

SELF-TALK, THE INNER dialogue we have with ourselves, plays a significant role in shaping our attitude. Positive self-talk can boost confidence, enhance performance, and improve overall mental health. Conversely, negative self-talk can undermine our self-esteem and hinder our ability to achieve our goals.

To develop a positive attitude, it is crucial to become aware of your self-talk and to actively challenge negative thoughts. When you catch yourself thinking, "I can't do this," try to reframe it to, "This is challenging, but I can learn and improve." By consistently practicing positive self-talk, you can build a more optimistic and resilient mindset.

Surround Yourself with Positivity

THE PEOPLE WE SPEND time with can significantly influence our attitude and outlook on life. Surrounding yourself with positive, supportive, and encouraging individuals can help you maintain a positive attitude. Seek out relationships that uplift and inspire you, and distance yourself from those that bring negativity and pessimism.

In addition to relationships, consider the impact of your environment. Create a space that inspires and motivates you. This could involve decorating your home or workspace with uplifting quotes, images, and reminders of your goals and accomplishments.

Practice Mindfulness and Stress Management

MINDFULNESS, THE PRACTICE of staying present and fully engaged in the current moment, can help reduce stress and promote a positive attitude. Mindfulness techniques, such as meditation, deep breathing, and mindful movement, can help you stay grounded and focused, even in challenging situations.

Stress management is also crucial for maintaining a positive attitude. Chronic stress can lead to burnout, negativity, and a pessimistic outlook. Develop healthy coping mechanisms, such as exercise, hobbies, and social connections, to manage stress and maintain a positive mindset.

Overcoming Negative Thought Patterns

NEGATIVE THOUGHT PATTERNS, such as catastrophizing, black-and-white thinking, and overgeneralization, can undermine our optimism and hinder our ability to achieve our goals. Overcoming these thought patterns requires awareness, effort, and practice.

Recognizing Negative Thought Patterns

THE FIRST STEP IN OVERCOMING negative thought patterns is recognizing them. Pay attention to your thoughts and identify any recurring patterns of negativity. Common negative thought patterns include:

- Catastrophizing: Expecting the worst possible outcome in any situation. For example, thinking, "If I make a mistake, I'll lose my job and never find another one."

- Black-and-White Thinking: Seeing situations in extremes, with no middle ground. For example, thinking, "If I'm not perfect, I'm a failure."

- Overgeneralization: Making broad conclusions based on a single event. For example, thinking, "I failed this test, so I'm terrible at everything."

Challenging Negative Thoughts

ONCE YOU HAVE IDENTIFIED negative thought patterns, the next step is to challenge them. Ask yourself whether these thoughts are based on facts or assumptions. Consider alternative explanations and perspectives. For example, if you are catastrophizing about a mistake at work, remind yourself of past successes and the steps you can take to rectify the situation.

It can also be helpful to practice self-compassion. Treat yourself with the same kindness and understanding that you would offer a friend. Recognize that everyone makes mistakes and that failure is a natural part of the learning process.

Replacing Negative Thoughts with Positive Ones

REPLACING NEGATIVE thoughts with positive ones involves consciously choosing to focus on more constructive and empowering thoughts. This does not mean ignoring or suppressing negative thoughts, but rather shifting your focus to more helpful perspectives.

For example, instead of thinking, "I'll never be able to do this," try thinking, "This is challenging, but I can take it one step at a time and ask for help if I need it." By consistently practicing this shift in focus, you can build a more optimistic and resilient mindset.

Building Resilience

RESILIENCE, THE ABILITY to bounce back from adversity, is a crucial component of an optimistic mindset. Building resilience involves developing skills and strategies to cope with challenges and setbacks.

One way to build resilience is to develop a growth mindset, as discussed earlier. Believing that you can learn and grow from challenges can help you stay motivated and persistent, even in difficult times.

Another strategy is to focus on your strengths. Identify your unique skills and talents, and find ways to leverage them in challenging situations. By focusing on what you can do, rather than what you can't, you can build confidence and resilience.

Seeking Support

FINALLY, REMEMBER THAT you do not have to overcome negative thought patterns alone. Seeking support from friends, family, or a mental health professional can provide valuable perspective and encouragement. Talking about your thoughts and feelings with someone you trust can help you gain insight and develop more constructive ways of thinking.

In conclusion, developing a mindset of optimism involves understanding and cultivating a growth mindset, developing a positive attitude, and overcoming negative thought patterns. By practicing these skills and strategies, you can build a more resilient and optimistic outlook on life, enhancing your ability to achieve your goals and find fulfillment.

Chapter 4: Techniques for Cultivating Positive Thoughts

Affirmations and Self-Talk

Affirmations and self-talk are powerful tools for cultivating positive thoughts and fostering a mindset of optimism. These techniques can help reshape your internal dialogue, boost self-esteem, and promote a more positive outlook on life.

The Power of Affirmations

AFFIRMATIONS ARE POSITIVE statements that you repeat to yourself to challenge and overcome negative thoughts and self-sabotage. They are rooted in the belief that by consistently affirming positive thoughts, you can influence your subconscious mind, which in turn affects your behavior, emotions, and overall mental state.

How Affirmations Work

AFFIRMATIONS WORK BY gradually replacing negative or unproductive thoughts with more positive and empowering ones. This process helps to rewire the brain, creating new neural pathways that support a more optimistic and confident mindset.

For example, if you often find yourself thinking, "I'm not good enough," you can use affirmations to counteract this belief. By consistently repeating a positive statement such as, "I am capable and worthy of success," you can begin to shift your mindset and cultivate a more positive self-image.

Crafting Effective Affirmations

TO CREATE EFFECTIVE affirmations, follow these guidelines:

1. Use Positive Language: Affirmations should be framed in positive terms. Instead of focusing on what you want to avoid, focus on what you want to achieve. For example, instead of saying, "I will not fail," say, "I am successful in all my endeavors."

2. Be Specific: The more specific your affirmations, the more impactful they will be. Tailor your affirmations to address your unique goals, challenges, and aspirations. For instance, "I am confident in my ability to lead successful projects at work" is more effective than a generic statement like, "I am confident."

3. Present Tense: Write affirmations in the present tense, as if they are already true. This helps to reinforce the belief that you are already embodying the qualities or achieving the outcomes you desire. For example, say, "I am healthy and energetic," rather than, "I will be healthy and energetic."

4. Emotionally Charged: Infuse your affirmations with emotion to enhance their impact. Use words that evoke strong, positive feelings and resonate with your personal values and desires. For example, "I am passionate about my work and thrive in my career" can evoke a stronger emotional response than a simple, "I am good at my job."

Incorporating Affirmations into Daily Life

TO MAXIMIZE THE EFFECTIVENESS of affirmations, incorporate them into your daily routine. Here are some practical ways to do this:

1. Morning Routine: Start your day with affirmations to set a positive tone for the rest of the day. Repeat your affirmations out loud or silently as you get ready in the morning.

2. Visualization: Combine affirmations with visualization techniques. As you repeat your affirmations, imagine yourself achieving your goals and embodying the qualities you desire. This creates a vivid mental image that reinforces your positive beliefs.

3. Written Affirmations: Write down your affirmations in a journal or on sticky notes placed around your home or workspace. Seeing these positive statements throughout the day serves as a constant reminder to maintain a positive mindset.

4. Affirmation Apps: Use smartphone apps designed to help you practice affirmations. These apps can send you daily reminders and prompts to repeat your affirmations, making it easier to stay consistent.

The Role of Self-Talk

SELF-TALK IS THE INTERNAL dialogue you have with yourself throughout the day. It can be positive and supportive, or negative and self-critical. The way you talk to yourself significantly influences your thoughts, emotions, and behaviors.

Understanding Negative Self-Talk

NEGATIVE SELF-TALK often manifests as automatic, habitual thoughts that undermine your confidence and well-being. Common forms of negative self-talk include:

1. Catastrophizing: Expecting the worst possible outcome in any situation. For example, thinking, "If I make a mistake, everything will fall apart."

2. Personalizing: Blaming yourself for events outside your control. For example, thinking, "It's my fault that the project failed, even though it was a team effort."

3. Overgeneralizing: Drawing broad, negative conclusions based on a single event. For example, thinking, "I failed this exam, so I'm a failure in all aspects of life."

4. Black-and-White Thinking: Viewing situations in extremes, with no middle ground. For example, thinking, "If I'm not perfect, I'm a total failure."

Transforming Negative Self-Talk

TO TRANSFORM NEGATIVE self-talk into positive self-talk, follow these steps:

1. Awareness: The first step is to become aware of your negative self-talk. Pay attention to your thoughts and identify any recurring negative patterns.

2. Challenge Negative Thoughts: Once you recognize negative self-talk, challenge these thoughts by questioning their validity. Ask yourself if they are based on facts or assumptions. Consider alternative, more positive perspectives.

3. Reframe with Positive Self-Talk: Replace negative thoughts with positive, empowering statements. For example, instead of thinking, "I'll never be able to do this," reframe it to, "This is challenging, but I can learn and improve with effort."

4. Practice Self-Compassion: Treat yourself with the same kindness and understanding that you would offer a friend. Recognize that everyone makes mistakes and that failure is a natural part of the learning process.

5. Consistency: Consistently practice positive self-talk to reinforce new, constructive thought patterns. The more you practice, the more natural and automatic positive self-talk will become.

Visualization and Mental Imagery

VISUALIZATION AND MENTAL imagery are techniques that involve creating vivid mental pictures of desired outcomes and experiences. These techniques can enhance performance, boost confidence, and promote a positive mindset by harnessing the power of imagination.

The Science Behind Visualization

RESEARCH HAS SHOWN that visualization can have a profound impact on the brain and body. When you visualize a specific scenario, your brain activates the same neural pathways as if you were actually experiencing it. This process helps to create a mental blueprint for success and can improve performance, reduce anxiety, and increase motivation.

Types of Visualization

THERE ARE SEVERAL TYPES of visualization techniques that can be used to cultivate positive thoughts:

1. Outcome Visualization: This involves imagining the successful completion of a goal or the achievement of a desired outcome. For example, an athlete might visualize crossing the finish line first, or a student might visualize receiving a high grade on an exam.

2. Process Visualization: This focuses on visualizing the steps and actions required to achieve a goal. For example, an athlete might visualize their training routine, or a student might visualize their study schedule and the process of completing assignments.

3. Healing Visualization: This technique involves imagining the body healing and recovering from illness or injury. It can be used to promote physical and emotional healing by creating a positive mental environment for recovery.

How to Practice Visualization

TO PRACTICE VISUALIZATION effectively, follow these steps:

1. Relaxation: Begin by finding a quiet, comfortable place where you can relax without distractions. Take a few deep breaths to calm your mind and body.

2. Detailed Imagery: Create a vivid mental image of your desired outcome or the process of achieving it. Use all your senses to make the visualization as realistic as possible. Imagine what you would see, hear, feel, smell, and even taste in that scenario.

3. Positive Emotions: Infuse your visualization with positive emotions. Imagine the joy, satisfaction, and pride you would feel upon achieving your goal. This helps to reinforce the positive mental state associated with the visualization.

4. Consistency: Practice visualization regularly to reinforce the mental blueprint. Aim to spend a few minutes each day visualizing your goals and desired outcomes.

5. Combine with Affirmations: Enhance your visualization practice by incorporating affirmations. As you visualize, repeat positive affirmations that reinforce your belief in your ability to achieve your goals.

Benefits of Visualization

VISUALIZATION OFFERS numerous benefits for cultivating positive thoughts and achieving success:

1. Enhanced Performance: Visualization can improve performance in various areas, including sports, academics, and professional endeavors. By mentally rehearsing successful outcomes, you can enhance your confidence and readiness to perform.

2. Increased Motivation: Visualizing your goals and desired outcomes can boost motivation and commitment. It helps to create a clear, compelling vision of what you want to achieve, making it easier to stay focused and driven.

3. Reduced Anxiety: Visualization can reduce anxiety by creating a sense of familiarity and preparedness. By mentally rehearsing challenging situations, you can alleviate fear and build confidence.

4. Positive Mindset: Visualization fosters a positive mindset by focusing on success and positive outcomes. It helps to counteract negative thoughts and create a more optimistic outlook on life.

Journaling and Gratitude Practices

JOURNALING AND GRATITUDE practices are powerful techniques for cultivating positive thoughts and enhancing overall well-being. These practices provide an opportunity to reflect on positive experiences, express gratitude, and gain insight into your thoughts and emotions.

The Benefits of Journaling

JOURNALING INVOLVES writing down your thoughts, feelings, and experiences on a regular basis. This practice can help you process emotions, gain clarity, and develop a more positive mindset.

Types of Journaling

THERE ARE SEVERAL TYPES of journaling that can be used to cultivate positive thoughts:

1. Reflective Journaling: This involves reflecting on your daily experiences and identifying positive moments, achievements, and lessons learned. It helps to shift your focus from negative events to positive ones.

2. Gratitude Journaling: This practice involves writing down things you are grateful for each day. It helps to cultivate a sense of appreciation and positivity by focusing on the good in your life.

3. Goal-Oriented Journaling: This type of journaling involves setting goals and tracking your progress. It helps to maintain motivation and celebrate achievements along the way.

4. Creative Journaling: This involves using creative expression, such as drawing, poetry, or storytelling, to explore your thoughts and emotions. It can be a fun and therapeutic way to cultivate positive thoughts.

How to Start a Journaling Practice

TO START A JOURNALING practice, follow these steps:

1. Choose a Medium: Decide whether you want to use a physical notebook or a digital journaling app. Choose a medium that feels comfortable and convenient for you.

2. Set a Routine: Establish a regular journaling routine, whether it's daily, weekly, or at specific times of the day. Consistency is key to reaping the benefits of journaling.

3. Create a Positive Environment: Find a quiet, comfortable place where you can journal without distractions. Create a positive atmosphere with calming music, candles, or anything else that helps you relax.

4. Start with Prompts: If you're not sure what to write about, use prompts to get started. For example, you can reflect on a positive experience from the day, write about something you're grateful for, or set intentions for the future.

5. Be Honest and Authentic: Write honestly and authentically about your thoughts and feelings. There is no right or wrong way to journal, so allow yourself to express whatever comes to mind.

The Power of Gratitude Practices

GRATITUDE PRACTICES involve intentionally focusing on the positive aspects of your life and expressing appreciation for them. Research has shown that gratitude can improve mental health, enhance relationships, and increase overall life satisfaction.

Gratitude Journaling

ONE OF THE MOST EFFECTIVE gratitude practices is gratitude journaling. This involves writing down things you are grateful for each day. Here are some tips for starting a gratitude journal:

1. Consistency: Make gratitude journaling a daily habit. Set aside a few minutes each day to reflect on and write down things you are grateful for.

2. Specificity: Be specific about what you are grateful for. Instead of writing, "I'm grateful for my family," try, "I'm grateful for the support and love my family shows me, especially when I'm going through tough times."

3. Positive Emotions: Focus on the positive emotions associated with your gratitude. Reflect on how these positive experiences make you feel and the impact they have on your life.

4. Variety: Try to identify different things to be grateful for each day. This helps to expand your awareness of the positive aspects of your life and prevents the practice from becoming repetitive.

Other Gratitude Practices

IN ADDITION TO GRATITUDE journaling, there are other gratitude practices that can help cultivate positive thoughts:

1. Gratitude Letters: Write letters of appreciation to people who have made a positive impact on your life. Expressing your gratitude in writing can deepen your sense of appreciation and strengthen your relationships.

2. Gratitude Meditation: Practice gratitude meditation by focusing on the things you are grateful for. As you meditate, visualize the positive experiences and people in your life, and allow yourself to feel the emotions of gratitude and appreciation.

3. Gratitude Jar: Create a gratitude jar by writing down things you are grateful for on small slips of paper and placing them in a jar. Over time, you can revisit these notes to remind yourself of the positive aspects of your life.

4. Gratitude Walks: Take a walk and focus on the things you are grateful for in your surroundings. This practice helps to connect with nature and appreciate the beauty and abundance around you.

The Impact of Gratitude on Well-Being

GRATITUDE PRACTICES offer numerous benefits for mental and emotional well-being:

1. Improved Mood: Focusing on gratitude can enhance positive emotions and improve overall mood. It helps to shift attention away from negative thoughts and increase feelings of happiness and contentment.

2. Enhanced Resilience: Gratitude can build resilience by promoting a positive outlook and helping to reframe challenging situations. It encourages a sense of hope and optimism, even in difficult times.

3. Strengthened Relationships: Expressing gratitude can strengthen relationships by fostering feelings of appreciation and connection. It helps to create a positive and supportive social environment.

4. Reduced Stress: Gratitude practices can reduce stress by promoting relaxation and positive thinking. They help to counteract the negative effects of stress and enhance overall well-being.

Integrating Positive Thought Techniques into Daily Life

TO CULTIVATE A LASTING positive mindset, it is essential to integrate these techniques into your daily life. By consistently practicing affirmations, visualization, journaling, and gratitude, you can create a foundation of positive thoughts that supports your overall well-being and success.

Creating a Positive Routine

ESTABLISHING A POSITIVE routine involves incorporating these techniques into your daily schedule. Here are some tips for creating a positive routine:

1. Morning Practice: Start your day with positive practices such as affirmations, visualization, and gratitude journaling. This sets a positive tone for the rest of the day and helps you begin with a mindset of optimism.

2. Midday Check-In: Take a break during the day to check in with yourself and practice positive self-talk. Reflect on your progress, celebrate small wins, and reframe any negative thoughts that may arise.

3. Evening Reflection: End your day with reflective journaling and gratitude practices. Reflect on the positive experiences of the day and express appreciation for the good things in your life.

Combining Techniques

COMBINING DIFFERENT positive thought techniques can enhance their effectiveness and create a comprehensive approach to cultivating positivity. For example, you can combine affirmations with visualization, or integrate gratitude journaling into your reflective journaling practice.

Staying Consistent

CONSISTENCY IS KEY to reaping the benefits of these techniques. Make a commitment to practice them regularly, even on days when you may not feel particularly positive. Over time, these practices will become habits that support your overall well-being.

Seeking Support

REMEMBER THAT YOU DO not have to cultivate positive thoughts alone. Seek support from friends, family, or a mentor who can encourage and motivate you. Joining a community or group focused on personal development and positivity can also provide valuable support and inspiration.

In conclusion, cultivating positive thoughts involves the consistent practice of techniques such as affirmations, self-talk, visualization, journaling, and gratitude. By integrating these practices into your daily life, you can create a foundation of positivity that enhances your overall well-being, resilience, and success.

Chapter 5: Overcoming Obstacles to Positive Thinking

Identifying and Challenging Limiting Beliefs

Limiting beliefs are deeply ingrained convictions that constrain our potential and hinder our ability to think positively. These beliefs often stem from past experiences, societal conditioning, and self-imposed limitations. Overcoming these obstacles requires recognizing and challenging these beliefs to create a more empowering mindset.

Understanding Limiting Beliefs

LIMITING BELIEFS ARE often subconscious and can manifest in various ways, such as self-doubt, fear of failure, and feelings of unworthiness. Common limiting beliefs include thoughts like "I'm not good enough," "I don't deserve success," and "I'm not capable of achieving my goals." These beliefs act as mental barriers that prevent us from pursuing our dreams and living to our fullest potential.

Origins of Limiting Beliefs

LIMITING BELIEFS CAN originate from several sources:

1. Childhood Experiences: Negative experiences and criticisms during childhood can shape our self-perception and lead to the formation of limiting beliefs. For instance, being told that you are not smart enough or capable can create a lasting impact on your self-esteem.

2. Cultural and Societal Influences: Societal norms and cultural expectations can also contribute to limiting beliefs. Stereotypes, gender roles, and societal pressures can shape our beliefs about what we can or cannot achieve.

3. Past Failures: Negative experiences and failures can reinforce limiting beliefs. When we encounter setbacks, we may start to believe that we are inherently incapable of success.

4. Self-Comparison: Comparing ourselves to others can lead to feelings of inadequacy and reinforce limiting beliefs. Seeing others succeed while perceiving ourselves as lacking can create a sense of unworthiness.

Identifying Limiting Beliefs

THE FIRST STEP IN OVERCOMING limiting beliefs is identifying them. This requires self-reflection and a willingness to examine our thoughts and behaviors. Here are some strategies to help identify limiting beliefs:

1. Self-Reflection: Take time to reflect on your thoughts and behaviors. Notice any recurring patterns of self-doubt, fear, or negative self-talk. Ask yourself, "What beliefs are driving these thoughts and behaviors?"

2. Journaling: Journaling can be a powerful tool for uncovering limiting beliefs. Write down your thoughts, feelings, and experiences, and look for patterns that reveal underlying beliefs.

3. Feedback from Others: Seek feedback from trusted friends, family members, or mentors. They can provide valuable insights into your beliefs and behaviors that you may not be aware of.

4. Mindfulness and Meditation: Practice mindfulness and meditation to become more aware of your thoughts and beliefs. These practices can help you observe your mental patterns without judgment and gain clarity on your limiting beliefs.

Challenging Limiting Beliefs

ONCE YOU HAVE IDENTIFIED your limiting beliefs, the next step is to challenge and reframe them. This process involves questioning the validity of these beliefs and replacing them with more empowering thoughts. Here are some strategies for challenging limiting beliefs:

1. Examine the Evidence: Evaluate the evidence supporting your limiting beliefs. Ask yourself, "Is this belief based on facts or assumptions?" Look for evidence that contradicts your belief and consider alternative perspectives.

2. Reframe Negative Thoughts: Reframe your limiting beliefs into positive, empowering statements. For example, instead of thinking, "I'm not good enough," reframe it to, "I am capable and worthy of success." Consistently practice this reframe to reinforce positive thinking.

3. Set Realistic Goals: Set small, achievable goals that challenge your limiting beliefs. As you achieve these goals, you will build confidence and start to see evidence that contradicts your limiting beliefs.

4. Visualize Success: Use visualization techniques to imagine yourself overcoming your limiting beliefs and achieving your goals. Visualization helps to create a mental blueprint for success and reinforces positive thinking.

5. Seek Support: Seek support from a coach, therapist, or support group. They can provide guidance, encouragement, and tools to help you challenge and overcome your limiting beliefs.

6. Practice Self-Compassion: Be kind and compassionate towards yourself. Recognize that everyone has limiting beliefs and that overcoming them is a process. Treat yourself with the same kindness and understanding that you would offer a friend.

Managing Stress and Anxiety

STRESS AND ANXIETY are common obstacles to positive thinking. They can cloud our judgment, reduce our resilience, and make it difficult to maintain an optimistic outlook. Managing stress and anxiety involves developing healthy coping mechanisms and strategies to promote mental well-being.

Understanding Stress and Anxiety

STRESS IS THE BODY'S response to perceived threats or challenges. It can be triggered by various factors, such as work pressure, personal relationships, financial concerns, and health issues. While short-term stress can be motivating, chronic stress can have detrimental effects on our physical and mental health.

Anxiety, on the other hand, is a persistent feeling of worry or fear that can interfere with daily life. It is often characterized by excessive worry, restlessness, irritability, and difficulty concentrating. Anxiety can stem from various sources, including genetic predisposition, environmental factors, and traumatic experiences.

The Impact of Stress and Anxiety on Positive Thinking

STRESS AND ANXIETY can significantly impact our ability to think positively. When we are stressed or anxious, our brain's focus shifts to survival mode, making it difficult to see the bigger picture or maintain an optimistic outlook. Chronic stress and anxiety can lead to negative thought patterns, self-doubt, and a sense of helplessness.

Strategies for Managing Stress

MANAGING STRESS INVOLVES adopting healthy habits and strategies to reduce its impact on our well-being. Here are some effective strategies for managing stress:

1. Exercise: Physical activity is one of the most effective ways to reduce stress. Exercise releases endorphins, which are natural mood enhancers. Regular exercise can help reduce tension, improve sleep, and boost overall well-being.

2. Mindfulness and Meditation: Mindfulness and meditation practices can help calm the mind and reduce stress. These practices involve focusing on the present moment and letting go of negative thoughts and worries. Techniques

such as deep breathing, progressive muscle relaxation, and guided meditation can be particularly effective.

3. Healthy Lifestyle: Maintaining a healthy lifestyle can help manage stress. This includes eating a balanced diet, getting enough sleep, and avoiding excessive consumption of caffeine and alcohol. A healthy body supports a healthy mind.

4. Time Management: Effective time management can help reduce stress by preventing overwhelm. Prioritize tasks, set realistic goals, and break larger tasks into smaller, manageable steps. Learn to delegate and say no when necessary.

5. Social Support: Connecting with friends, family, and support groups can provide emotional support and help alleviate stress. Talking about your feelings and experiences with others can provide perspective and reduce feelings of isolation.

6. Hobbies and Interests: Engaging in hobbies and activities that you enjoy can provide a sense of relaxation and fulfillment. Whether it's reading, gardening, painting, or playing a musical instrument, find activities that bring you joy and make time for them regularly.

7. Professional Help: If stress becomes overwhelming, consider seeking professional help. A therapist or counselor can provide tools and techniques to manage stress and address underlying issues.

Strategies for Managing Anxiety

MANAGING ANXIETY INVOLVES developing coping mechanisms and strategies to reduce its impact on daily life. Here are some effective strategies for managing anxiety:

1. Cognitive Behavioral Therapy (CBT): CBT is a therapeutic approach that helps individuals identify and challenge negative thought patterns and behaviors. It can be particularly effective for managing anxiety by providing tools to reframe anxious thoughts and develop healthier coping strategies.

2. Relaxation Techniques: Relaxation techniques, such as deep breathing, progressive muscle relaxation, and guided imagery, can help reduce anxiety. These techniques promote a state of calm and relaxation, which can counteract the physical and mental symptoms of anxiety.

3. Mindfulness and Meditation: Mindfulness and meditation practices can help reduce anxiety by promoting present-moment awareness and acceptance. Techniques such as mindful breathing, body scan meditation, and loving-kindness meditation can be particularly effective.

4. Healthy Lifestyle: Maintaining a healthy lifestyle can help manage anxiety. This includes regular exercise, a balanced diet, and sufficient sleep. Avoiding caffeine and alcohol can also reduce anxiety symptoms.

5. Journaling: Journaling can be a powerful tool for managing anxiety. Writing down your thoughts and feelings can help you process emotions, gain clarity, and identify triggers. It can also provide a sense of release and relief.

6. Exposure Therapy: Exposure therapy involves gradually exposing yourself to anxiety-provoking situations in a controlled and safe manner. This can help desensitize you to the triggers and reduce the intensity of anxiety over time.

7. Professional Help: If anxiety becomes overwhelming, consider seeking professional help. A therapist or counselor can provide tools and techniques to manage anxiety and address underlying issues. Medication may also be prescribed in some cases to help manage symptoms.

Building Resilience to Stress and Anxiety

BUILDING RESILIENCE involves developing the ability to adapt and bounce back from stress and anxiety. Here are some strategies to build resilience:

1. Positive Thinking: Cultivate a positive mindset by focusing on your strengths, achievements, and the positive aspects of your life. Practice gratitude and affirmations to reinforce positive thinking.

2. Problem-Solving Skills: Develop effective problem-solving skills to address challenges and stressors. Break down problems into smaller, manageable steps and focus on finding solutions rather than dwelling on the problem.

3. Emotional Regulation: Learn to regulate your emotions through techniques such as mindfulness, deep breathing, and cognitive reframing. Recognize and acknowledge your emotions without judgment and find healthy ways to express and manage them.

4. Social Connections: Build and maintain strong social connections. Surround yourself with supportive and positive individuals who can provide emotional support and encouragement.

5. Self-Care: Prioritize self-care by making time for activities that promote relaxation and well-being. This includes physical exercise, hobbies, relaxation techniques, and spending time in nature.

6. Flexibility and Adaptability: Develop the ability to adapt to change and uncertainty. Embrace a flexible mindset and be open to new perspectives and solutions. This can help you navigate stress and anxiety with greater ease.

Coping with Setbacks and Failures

SETBACKS AND FAILURES are inevitable parts of life. How we respond to these challenges significantly impacts our ability to maintain a positive mindset. Coping with setbacks and failures involves developing resilience, learning from experiences, and staying motivated.

Understanding the Impact of Setbacks and Failures

SETBACKS AND FAILURES can trigger negative emotions such as disappointment, frustration, and self-doubt. They can shake our confidence and make it difficult to stay positive. However, setbacks and failures also provide valuable opportunities for growth and learning.

The Role of Mindset

OUR MINDSET PLAYS A crucial role in how we respond to setbacks and failures. A growth mindset, as discussed in Chapter 3, allows us to view challenges as opportunities for learning and development. In contrast, a fixed mindset can lead to feelings of defeat and helplessness.

Embracing Failure as a Learning Opportunity

TO COPE WITH SETBACKS and failures, it is essential to shift our perspective and embrace failure as a learning opportunity. Here are some strategies to help you do this:

1. Reframe Failure: Reframe failure as a natural part of the learning process. Recognize that setbacks and failures are not indicators of your worth or abilities but opportunities for growth and improvement.

2. Analyze and Learn: Take time to analyze the setback or failure and identify what went wrong. Ask yourself, "What can I learn from this experience?" Use the insights gained to make improvements and avoid similar mistakes in the future.

3. Focus on Effort and Improvement: Instead of dwelling on the outcome, focus on the effort you put in and the progress you made. Celebrate small wins and acknowledge your hard work and dedication.

4. Maintain a Growth Mindset: Cultivate a growth mindset by embracing challenges, persisting through obstacles, and viewing effort as a path to mastery. Remind yourself that your abilities can develop and improve with practice and perseverance.

Building Resilience to Setbacks and Failures

BUILDING RESILIENCE involves developing the ability to bounce back from setbacks and failures. Here are some strategies to build resilience:

1. Positive Self-Talk: Practice positive self-talk to counteract negative thoughts and self-doubt. Remind yourself of your strengths, achievements, and the progress you have made.

2. Set Realistic Goals: Set realistic and achievable goals that challenge you without overwhelming you. Break larger goals into smaller, manageable steps and celebrate your progress along the way.

3. Seek Support: Seek support from friends, family, mentors, or support groups. Sharing your experiences and receiving encouragement and guidance can help you stay motivated and resilient.

4. Develop Coping Strategies: Develop healthy coping strategies to manage stress and emotions. This includes mindfulness, relaxation techniques, exercise, and engaging in hobbies and activities that bring you joy.

5. Stay Flexible: Stay flexible and adaptable in the face of setbacks and failures. Be open to new perspectives and solutions, and be willing to adjust your approach as needed.

6. Maintain Perspective: Keep setbacks and failures in perspective. Remind yourself that they are temporary and do not define your worth or potential. Focus on the bigger picture and your long-term goals.

Staying Motivated in the Face of Setbacks

STAYING MOTIVATED IN the face of setbacks and failures requires maintaining a positive mindset and staying focused on your goals. Here are some strategies to help you stay motivated:

1. Reconnect with Your Why: Reconnect with your purpose and the reasons why you set your goals in the first place. Remind yourself of the bigger picture and the impact you want to make.

2. Visualize Success: Use visualization techniques to imagine yourself overcoming setbacks and achieving your goals. Visualize the positive outcomes and the emotions associated with success.

3. Set Milestones: Set small milestones and celebrate your progress along the way. This helps to maintain motivation and provides a sense of achievement.

4. Stay Flexible: Be willing to adjust your approach and try new strategies if something isn't working. Stay open to feedback and be adaptable in the face of challenges.

5. Surround Yourself with Positivity: Surround yourself with positive and supportive individuals who encourage and motivate you. Seek out role models and mentors who inspire you.

6. Practice Self-Care: Prioritize self-care to maintain your physical and mental well-being. This includes getting enough rest, eating a balanced diet, exercising, and engaging in activities that bring you joy.

Conclusion

OVERCOMING OBSTACLES to positive thinking involves identifying and challenging limiting beliefs, managing stress and anxiety, and coping with setbacks and failures. By developing strategies to address these challenges, you can cultivate a more positive mindset and enhance your overall well-being and resilience. Remember that overcoming these obstacles is a process that requires patience, self-compassion, and consistent effort. By embracing a growth mindset, practicing self-care, and seeking support, you can navigate challenges with greater ease and continue to move forward towards your goals.

Chapter 6: Positive Thinking in Daily Life

Incorporating Optimism into Your Routine

Integrating positive thinking into your daily routine can transform your life, making you more resilient, happier, and more successful. By consciously incorporating optimism into your day-to-day activities, you can foster a positive mindset that will influence every aspect of your life.

Morning Routine: Starting the Day Right

THE WAY YOU START YOUR day sets the tone for the rest of it. Establishing a morning routine that promotes positivity can help you begin each day with a positive outlook.

1. Wake Up Early

WAKING UP EARLY ALLOWS you to have a calm and unhurried start to your day. It gives you time to engage in activities that promote a positive mindset, such as meditation, exercise, or reading.

2. Practice Gratitude

BEGIN YOUR DAY BY ACKNOWLEDGING the things you are grateful for. This can be done through a gratitude journal where you write down three things you are thankful for each morning. Focusing on gratitude helps shift your mind towards positivity and abundance.

3. Positive Affirmations

INCORPORATE POSITIVE affirmations into your morning routine. These are statements that reinforce your self-worth and potential. For example, "I am capable of achieving my goals" or "Today will be a productive and fulfilling day." Repeating affirmations can set a positive tone for your day.

4. Mindfulness or Meditation

STARTING YOUR DAY WITH mindfulness or meditation can help you remain centered and calm. These practices allow you to focus on the present moment, reducing stress and promoting a positive mindset. Even a few minutes of deep breathing exercises can make a significant difference.

5. Physical Exercise

ENGAGING IN PHYSICAL activity in the morning releases endorphins, the body's natural mood lifters. Whether it's a full workout, a short jog, or some yoga stretches, exercise can boost your energy levels and enhance your mood for the day.

Throughout the Day: Maintaining Positivity

MAINTAINING A POSITIVE mindset throughout the day requires conscious effort and practice. Here are strategies to help you stay optimistic as you navigate daily challenges.

1. Positive Self-Talk

MONITOR YOUR INTERNAL dialogue and practice positive self-talk. When negative thoughts arise, counter them with positive statements. For example, if you catch yourself thinking, "I can't handle this," reframe it to, "I am capable of finding a solution."

2. Break Tasks into Manageable Steps

LARGE TASKS CAN FEEL overwhelming and lead to negative thinking. Break tasks into smaller, manageable steps and focus on completing them one at a time. This approach makes tasks seem less daunting and gives you a sense of accomplishment as you complete each step.

3. Take Regular Breaks

TAKING REGULAR BREAKS throughout the day helps to reduce stress and maintain a positive mindset. Use break time to stretch, take a walk, or engage in a quick mindfulness exercise. This can refresh your mind and prevent burnout.

4. Practice Random Acts of Kindness

ENGAGING IN ACTS OF kindness can boost your mood and promote positive thinking. Simple gestures like complimenting a colleague, helping someone in need, or expressing gratitude can create a positive ripple effect.

5. Stay Organized

KEEPING YOUR ENVIRONMENT organized can reduce stress and promote positivity. A clutter-free workspace and home can create a sense of order and calm, making it easier to maintain a positive mindset.

6. Focus on Solutions

WHEN FACED WITH CHALLENGES, focus on finding solutions rather than dwelling on problems. Approach obstacles with a problem-solving mindset and view them as opportunities for growth and learning.

Evening Routine: Ending the Day Positively

ENDING YOUR DAY ON a positive note can enhance your overall well-being and set the stage for a good night's sleep. Incorporate these practices into your evening routine to foster positivity.

1. Reflect on the Day

TAKE A FEW MINUTES each evening to reflect on your day. Consider what went well, what you accomplished, and what you learned. This practice helps you focus on the positives and acknowledge your efforts.

2. Gratitude Journal

CONTINUING YOUR GRATITUDE practice in the evening can reinforce a positive mindset. Write down three things you are grateful for that happened during the day. Reflecting on positive experiences can improve your mood and promote restful sleep.

3. Unplug and Relax

SPEND SOME TIME UNPLUGGING from electronic devices and winding down before bed. Engage in relaxing activities such as reading, taking a warm bath, or practicing gentle stretches. Creating a calm evening routine can help you relax and prepare for a good night's sleep.

4. Set Intentions for Tomorrow

BEFORE GOING TO BED, set positive intentions for the next day. Think about what you want to accomplish and how you want to approach the day. This practice can help you wake up with a sense of purpose and positivity.

Positive Communication and Interactions

EFFECTIVE COMMUNICATION and positive interactions with others are crucial for maintaining a positive mindset. How we communicate and interact with others can significantly influence our mood and overall well-being.

The Power of Positive Communication

POSITIVE COMMUNICATION involves expressing yourself in a way that is respectful, constructive, and uplifting. It fosters healthy relationships and creates a positive social environment.

1. Active Listening

ACTIVE LISTENING IS a key component of positive communication. It involves fully focusing on the speaker, understanding their message, and responding thoughtfully. Practice active listening by maintaining eye contact, nodding, and providing verbal affirmations.

2. Positive Language

USE POSITIVE LANGUAGE when communicating with others. Avoid negative or critical remarks and focus on constructive and encouraging words. For example, instead of saying, "You did that wrong," try saying, "Here's a different approach that might work better."

3. Express Appreciation

REGULARLY EXPRESS APPRECIATION and gratitude towards others. Acknowledge their efforts, contributions, and positive qualities. Simple gestures like saying "thank you" or complimenting someone's work can foster a positive and supportive atmosphere.

4. Empathy and Understanding

PRACTICE EMPATHY BY trying to understand others' perspectives and feelings. Show compassion and support when others are facing challenges. Empathy strengthens relationships and promotes a sense of connection and positivity.

5. Non-Verbal Communication

PAY ATTENTION TO YOUR non-verbal communication, such as body language, facial expressions, and tone of voice. Ensure that your non-verbal cues align with your positive verbal messages. For example, a warm smile and open posture can enhance positive communication.

Building Positive Relationships

HEALTHY, POSITIVE RELATIONSHIPS are essential for overall well-being and a positive mindset. Building and maintaining these relationships requires effort and intentionality.

1. Quality Time

Spend quality time with loved ones, friends, and colleagues. Engage in activities that you enjoy together and create meaningful experiences. Quality time fosters connection and strengthens relationships.

2. Open Communication

Maintain open and honest communication with the people in your life. Share your thoughts, feelings, and experiences, and encourage others to do the same. Open communication builds trust and mutual understanding.

3. Support and Encouragement

Provide support and encouragement to others, especially during challenging times. Offer a listening ear, words of encouragement, or practical help. Being a source of support can strengthen relationships and create a positive social environment.

4. Resolve Conflicts Constructively

Conflicts are a natural part of any relationship. When conflicts arise, address them constructively. Focus on finding solutions rather than assigning blame. Practice active listening, express your feelings calmly, and work towards a resolution that benefits both parties.

5. Celebrate Successes

Celebrate the successes and achievements of those around you. Whether it's a small victory or a major accomplishment, acknowledging and celebrating others' successes fosters positivity and strengthens relationships.

Creating a Positive Environment

YOUR ENVIRONMENT PLAYS a significant role in shaping your mindset and overall well-being. Creating a positive environment at home, work, and in your social circles can enhance your ability to think positively and maintain a sense of well-being.

Home Environment

YOUR HOME IS YOUR SANCTUARY, and creating a positive home environment can have a profound impact on your mindset.

1. Declutter and Organize

A cluttered and disorganized space can create stress and negatively impact your mood. Take time to declutter and organize your home. Keep only the items that bring you joy and serve a purpose. A tidy space can promote a sense of calm and positivity.

2. Personalize Your Space

Personalize your home with items that inspire and uplift you. This could include artwork, photographs, plants, or meaningful mementos. Surround yourself with things that bring you joy and reflect your personality.

3. Natural Light and Fresh Air

Maximize natural light and fresh air in your home. Open windows, use light-colored curtains, and arrange furniture to allow sunlight to fill the space. Natural light and fresh air can boost your mood and energy levels.

4. Create Relaxation Zones

Designate areas in your home for relaxation and self-care. This could be a cozy reading nook, a meditation corner, or a space for hobbies and activities you enjoy. Having a dedicated space for relaxation can help you unwind and recharge.

5. Positive Affirmations and Quotes

Display positive affirmations and quotes around your home. Place them in areas where you will see them frequently, such as on the fridge, bathroom mirror, or workspace. These reminders can reinforce a positive mindset.

Work Environment

CREATING A POSITIVE work environment is essential for maintaining productivity, motivation, and overall well-being.

1. Organize Your Workspace

Keep your workspace organized and clutter-free. Use storage solutions to keep supplies and documents neatly arranged. A clean and organized workspace can reduce stress and improve focus.

2. Personalize Your Desk

Personalize your desk with items that inspire you and make you feel comfortable. This could include family photos, motivational quotes, or plants. Personal touches can create a positive and inviting workspace.

3. Take Breaks

Regular breaks are essential for maintaining productivity and reducing stress. Take short breaks throughout the day to stretch, walk, or simply relax. Use break time to recharge and clear your mind.

4. Positive Interactions with Colleagues

Foster positive interactions with your colleagues. Practice active listening, express appreciation, and offer support and encouragement. Building positive relationships at work can create a supportive and collaborative environment.

5. Set Boundaries

Set clear boundaries between work and personal life. Avoid overworking and ensure you have time for relaxation and self-care outside of work hours. Maintaining a healthy work-life balance is crucial for overall well-being.

Social Environment

YOUR SOCIAL ENVIRONMENT, including your relationships and social activities, significantly influences your mindset and well-being.

1. Choose Positive Influences

Surround yourself with positive and supportive individuals who uplift and inspire you. Limit interactions with people who bring negativity or drain your energy. Positive social connections can enhance your mood and overall outlook.

2. Engage in Meaningful Activities

Participate in activities and social events that bring you joy and fulfillment. Whether it's volunteering, joining a club, or attending social gatherings, engaging in meaningful activities can foster a sense of purpose and positivity.

3. Practice Kindness and Generosity

Practice acts of kindness and generosity towards others. This could include volunteering, helping a friend in need, or simply offering a kind word. Acts of kindness can create a positive ripple effect and enhance your own sense of well-being.

4. Build a Support Network

Build a support network of friends, family, and mentors who can provide guidance, encouragement, and support. A strong support network can help you navigate challenges and celebrate successes.

5. Limit Exposure to Negativity

Limit your exposure to negative influences, such as negative news, toxic relationships, and social media negativity. Be mindful of the content you consume and the people you interact with. Focus on positive and uplifting influences.

Creating a Positive Mindset Through Self-Care

SELF-CARE IS AN ESSENTIAL component of maintaining a positive mindset. Prioritizing self-care can enhance your physical, mental, and emotional well-being.

1. Physical Self-Care

Take care of your physical health through regular exercise, a balanced diet, and sufficient sleep. Physical self-care can boost your energy levels, improve your mood, and enhance your overall well-being.

2. Mental Self-Care

Engage in activities that stimulate and challenge your mind. This could include reading, learning new skills, or solving puzzles. Mental self-care promotes cognitive health and can enhance your sense of accomplishment.

3. Emotional Self-Care

Take time to process and express your emotions. Practice mindfulness, journaling, or talking to a trusted friend or therapist. Emotional self-care helps you manage stress and maintain emotional balance.

4. Spiritual Self-Care

Nurture your spiritual well-being through practices that align with your beliefs and values. This could include meditation, prayer, or spending time in nature. Spiritual self-care can provide a sense of purpose and inner peace.

5. Social Self-Care

Prioritize social connections and relationships that bring you joy and fulfillment. Spend quality time with loved ones, engage in social activities, and build a supportive network. Social self-care enhances your sense of belonging and positivity.

Conclusion

Incorporating positive thinking into your daily life involves intentional practices and habits that promote optimism, well-being, and resilience. By establishing a positive morning routine, maintaining positivity throughout the day, and ending the day on a positive note, you can create a foundation of positivity. Positive communication and interactions with others, along with creating a positive environment at home, work, and in your social circles, further enhance your ability to think positively. Prioritizing self-care in all its forms supports your overall well-being and helps you maintain a positive mindset. By integrating these practices into your daily life, you can cultivate a lasting sense of positivity and fulfillment.

Chapter 7: Positive Thinking and Emotional Intelligence

Understanding Emotional Intelligence

Emotional intelligence (EI), often referred to as emotional quotient (EQ), is the ability to recognize, understand, manage, and influence our own emotions and the emotions of others. Daniel Goleman, a psychologist, popularized this concept in the mid-1990s, highlighting its crucial role in personal and professional success. Unlike IQ, which measures cognitive abilities, EQ encompasses skills that relate to emotional awareness and interpersonal relationships.

The Five Components of Emotional Intelligence

GOLEMAN IDENTIFIES five key components of emotional intelligence:

1. Self-Awareness: The ability to recognize and understand your own emotions, strengths, weaknesses, values, and motives. Self-aware individuals are conscious of their emotional states and the impact these have on their thoughts and behavior.

2. Self-Regulation: The ability to manage and control your emotional responses. This includes handling stress, staying calm under pressure, and maintaining composure. Self-regulation allows individuals to think before acting and to express emotions appropriately.

3. Motivation: The drive to pursue goals with energy, persistence, and enthusiasm. Emotionally intelligent people are motivated by internal factors such as passion, curiosity, and the desire for personal growth, rather than external rewards.

4. Empathy: The ability to understand and share the feelings of others. Empathy involves recognizing emotional cues in others, appreciating different perspectives, and responding compassionately to their needs and concerns.

5. Social Skills: The ability to build and maintain healthy relationships. This includes effective communication, conflict resolution, teamwork, and leadership skills. Socially skilled individuals can navigate social complexities and foster positive interactions.

The Importance of Emotional Intelligence

EMOTIONAL INTELLIGENCE plays a significant role in various aspects of life, including personal well-being, relationships, and professional success. Here's why EQ is important:

- Personal Well-Being: High EQ contributes to better mental health, resilience, and overall happiness. Emotionally intelligent individuals can manage stress effectively, maintain a positive outlook, and navigate life's challenges with greater ease.

- *lRelationships: EQ enhances the quality of interpersonal relationships. It enables individuals to communicate effectively, resolve conflicts, and build strong, supportive connections with others.

- Professional Success: In the workplace, EQ is linked to better leadership, teamwork, and performance. Emotionally intelligent employees are more adaptable, collaborative, and capable of handling complex social dynamics.

Enhancing Self-Awareness and Self-Regulation

SELF-AWARENESS AND self-regulation are foundational aspects of emotional intelligence. Developing these skills can significantly enhance your ability to think positively and respond effectively to various situations.

Enhancing Self-Awareness

SELF-AWARENESS INVOLVES a deep understanding of your emotions, strengths, weaknesses, values, and motives. Here are some strategies to enhance self-awareness:

1. Reflective Practices

Regular self-reflection is essential for developing self-awareness. Set aside time each day to reflect on your experiences, thoughts, and emotions. Consider what triggered certain emotions and how you responded to them. Reflective practices can include journaling, meditation, or simply taking a few minutes of quiet contemplation.

2. Seek Feedback

Feedback from others can provide valuable insights into your behavior and emotional responses. Ask trusted friends, family members, or colleagues for their perspectives on your strengths and areas for improvement. Be open to constructive feedback and use it as an opportunity for growth.

3. Mindfulness and Meditation

Mindfulness practices, such as meditation, can help you become more aware of your thoughts and emotions. Mindfulness involves paying attention to the present moment without judgment. Regular mindfulness practice can enhance your ability to observe your emotional states and understand their impact on your behavior.

4. Personality Assessments

Personality assessments, such as the Myers-Briggs Type Indicator (MBTI) or the Big Five Personality Traits, can provide insights into your personality and emotional tendencies. Understanding your personality traits can help you become more aware of how you typically respond to different situations.

5. Emotional Tracking

Track your emotions throughout the day to identify patterns and triggers. Use a journal or an app to record your emotional states and the events that led to them. Reviewing your emotional tracking can help you gain a deeper understanding of your emotional responses.

Enhancing Self-Regulation

SELF-REGULATION INVOLVES managing your emotional responses to maintain control and express emotions appropriately. Here are some strategies to enhance self-regulation:

1. Develop Coping Strategies

Effective coping strategies can help you manage stress and emotional reactions. Techniques such as deep breathing, progressive muscle relaxation, and visualization can help you stay calm and composed in challenging situations.

2. Practice Delayed Gratification

Delayed gratification involves resisting immediate temptations in favor of long-term rewards. Practicing delayed gratification can strengthen your self-control and impulse regulation. Start with small exercises, such as waiting a few minutes before eating a treat, and gradually increase the difficulty.

3. Set Boundaries

Setting boundaries is crucial for maintaining emotional well-being. Learn to say no to requests or situations that may overwhelm you. Establishing clear boundaries helps you manage your time and energy effectively, reducing stress and enhancing self-regulation.

4. Manage Negative Emotions

Identify and manage negative emotions, such as anger, frustration, and anxiety. When you feel these emotions arising, take a moment to pause and breathe deeply. Acknowledge the emotion without judgment and consider the best way to respond. Techniques such as cognitive reframing and positive self-talk can help shift negative emotions to a more positive state.

5. Practice Emotional Detachment

Emotional detachment involves stepping back from your emotions to gain perspective. When faced with a challenging situation, try to observe your emotions from an outsider's viewpoint. This can help you respond more rationally and prevent emotional reactions from taking over.

Building Empathy and Social Skills

EMPATHY AND SOCIAL skills are essential components of emotional intelligence that enhance interpersonal relationships and foster positive interactions. Developing these skills can improve your ability to connect with others and create a supportive social environment.

Building Empathy

EMPATHY IS THE ABILITY to understand and share the feelings of others. It involves recognizing emotional cues, appreciating different perspectives, and responding compassionately. Here are some strategies to build empathy:

1. Active Listening

Active listening is a fundamental aspect of empathy. It involves fully focusing on the speaker, understanding their message, and responding thoughtfully. Practice active listening by maintaining eye contact, nodding, and providing verbal affirmations. Avoid interrupting and allow the speaker to express themselves fully.

2. Perspective-Taking

Perspective-taking involves imagining yourself in someone else's situation to understand their feelings and viewpoints. When interacting with others, try to put yourself in their shoes and consider how they might be feeling. This can enhance your ability to empathize and respond compassionately.

3. Emotional Validation

Emotional validation involves acknowledging and accepting another person's emotions. Instead of dismissing or minimizing their feelings, validate their emotions by saying things like, "I understand why you feel that way" or "It's okay to feel upset." Emotional validation shows that you respect and appreciate their emotional experience.

4. Non-Verbal Communication

Pay attention to non-verbal cues, such as body language, facial expressions, and tone of voice. These cues can provide valuable information about a person's emotional state. Responding to non-verbal cues with empathy can enhance your ability to connect with others on an emotional level.

5. Practice Compassion

Compassion involves showing kindness and understanding towards others, especially during difficult times. Practice acts of compassion, such as offering support, lending a listening ear, or providing assistance. Compassionate actions can strengthen your empathetic abilities and foster positive relationships.

Enhancing Social Skills

SOCIAL SKILLS ARE ESSENTIAL for building and maintaining healthy relationships. They include effective communication, conflict resolution, teamwork, and leadership abilities. Here are some strategies to enhance social skills:

1. Effective Communication

Effective communication involves expressing yourself clearly and listening to others. Practice clear and concise communication, using "I" statements to express your feelings and needs. Avoid blaming or criticizing others and focus on constructive dialogue.

2. Conflict Resolution

Conflict is a natural part of any relationship. Developing conflict resolution skills can help you navigate disagreements and find mutually beneficial solutions. Practice active listening, empathize with the other person's perspective, and seek common ground. Aim to resolve conflicts peacefully and collaboratively.

3. Teamwork

Teamwork involves collaborating with others to achieve common goals. Develop teamwork skills by being open to different viewpoints, sharing responsibilities, and supporting your team members. Effective teamwork fosters a positive and productive work environment.

4. Leadership

Leadership skills involve inspiring and guiding others towards a shared vision. Develop leadership abilities by setting a positive example, providing constructive feedback, and encouraging growth and development. Effective leaders create an environment of trust and respect.

5. Building Rapport

Building rapport involves creating a positive and trusting relationship with others. Practice building rapport by showing genuine interest in others, finding common ground, and being authentic. Strong rapport enhances social connections and fosters positive interactions.

Integrating Emotional Intelligence into Daily Life

INTEGRATING EMOTIONAL intelligence into your daily life can enhance your overall well-being and improve your relationships. Here are some practical ways to incorporate EQ into your routine:

1. Start with Self-Awareness

Begin each day with a self-awareness practice, such as journaling or meditation. Reflect on your emotions, thoughts, and intentions for the day. Set positive intentions and goals that align with your values and strengths.

2. Practice Mindfulness

Incorporate mindfulness into your daily routine to stay present and aware of your emotions. Practice mindful breathing, body scans, or mindful walking. Mindfulness helps you stay grounded and responsive rather than reactive.

3. Foster Positive Relationships

Make an effort to foster positive relationships with the people around you. Show appreciation, offer support, and practice empathy. Strong social connections enhance your emotional well-being and create a positive environment.

4. Develop Emotional Resilience

Develop emotional resilience by practicing self-regulation and coping strategies. When faced with challenges, use techniques such as deep breathing, positive self-talk, and cognitive reframing to maintain emotional balance.

5. Continuous Learning

Commit to continuous learning and personal growth. Seek opportunities to develop your emotional intelligence skills, such as workshops, books, or courses. Stay open to feedback and use it as a tool for improvement.

Conclusion

Emotional intelligence is a vital component of positive thinking and overall well-being. By enhancing self-awareness, self-regulation, empathy, and social skills, you can navigate life's challenges with greater ease and build stronger, more fulfilling relationships. Integrating emotional intelligence into your daily life involves intentional practices and habits that promote emotional awareness and positive interactions. By cultivating these skills, you can create a foundation of positivity and resilience that supports your personal and professional success.

Chapter 8: The Role of Positive Thinking in Physical Health

The Mind-Body Connection

The intricate relationship between the mind and body has been a topic of interest for centuries, with increasing scientific evidence supporting the profound impact that mental states can have on physical health. The concept of the mind-body connection posits that our thoughts, feelings, and attitudes can influence our biological functioning. This chapter delves into how positive thinking, as a mental state, can play a crucial role in enhancing physical health.

The mind-body connection is grounded in the understanding that psychological processes can affect physiological responses. For instance, when we experience stress, our bodies react by releasing stress hormones such as cortisol and adrenaline. These hormones prepare the body for a fight-or-flight response, which is beneficial in short-term, acute situations. However, chronic stress can lead to prolonged exposure to these hormones, resulting in adverse health outcomes such as weakened immune function, increased blood pressure, and heightened risk of chronic diseases like heart disease and diabetes.

Conversely, positive thinking can elicit beneficial physiological responses. Positive emotions and attitudes can promote the release of endorphins and other neurochemicals that enhance mood and well-being. These chemicals can reduce pain perception, improve immune function, and foster faster recovery from illness. Studies have shown that individuals with a positive outlook on life tend to have lower levels of inflammation and better overall physical health compared to those with a negative mindset.

The placebo effect is a well-documented phenomenon that exemplifies the power of the mind over the body. When patients believe that they are receiving a beneficial treatment, even if it is an inert substance, they often experience real improvements in their symptoms. This effect underscores the potential for positive thinking to bring about tangible health benefits.

Stress Reduction Techniques

STRESS IS AN INEVITABLE part of life, but how we manage it can significantly influence our physical health. Chronic stress can take a severe toll on the body, leading to a range of health problems. Therefore, incorporating effective stress reduction techniques is essential for maintaining physical health. Positive thinking plays a pivotal role in many of these techniques.

1. Mindfulness and Meditation: Mindfulness and meditation practices involve focusing the mind on the present moment, which can help reduce stress and promote relaxation. These practices encourage a non-judgmental awareness of thoughts and feelings, allowing individuals to cultivate a positive mindset. Regular mindfulness meditation has been shown to lower cortisol levels, reduce blood pressure, and improve immune function. By fostering a state of calm and positivity, mindfulness can mitigate the negative effects of stress on the body.

2. Deep Breathing Exercises: Deep breathing exercises, such as diaphragmatic breathing, can activate the body's relaxation response, counteracting the stress response. These exercises promote oxygen exchange and can help reduce feelings of anxiety and tension. Integrating positive affirmations with deep breathing can enhance the benefits, as focusing on positive thoughts can further alleviate stress and improve overall well-being.

3. Physical Activity: Regular physical activity is a powerful stress reducer. Exercise stimulates the release of endorphins, which are natural mood lifters. Engaging in activities that bring joy and satisfaction can amplify the positive effects of exercise on mental health. Whether it's a brisk walk, yoga, dancing, or playing a sport, finding an enjoyable form of physical activity can help manage stress and boost positive thinking.

4. Progressive Muscle Relaxation (PMR): PMR is a technique that involves tensing and then slowly relaxing each muscle group in the body. This practice

helps to reduce physical tension and promote relaxation. By focusing on the sensations of tension and release, individuals can become more attuned to their bodies and develop a greater sense of control over stress. Incorporating positive imagery and affirmations during PMR can enhance its effectiveness in reducing stress.

5. Creative Expression: Engaging in creative activities such as painting, writing, music, or crafting can serve as a therapeutic outlet for stress. Creative expression allows individuals to channel their emotions in a positive and constructive manner. The act of creating something beautiful or meaningful can foster a sense of accomplishment and positivity, reducing stress and promoting well-being.

6. Social Support: Building and maintaining strong social connections is crucial for stress management. Positive relationships provide emotional support, reduce feelings of isolation, and increase resilience to stress. Sharing experiences and discussing challenges with trusted friends or family members can provide new perspectives and encouragement, fostering a positive outlook.

7. Cognitive Behavioral Techniques: Cognitive-behavioral techniques involve identifying and challenging negative thought patterns and replacing them with more positive and realistic thoughts. This approach can help individuals develop healthier coping strategies and reduce stress. Techniques such as cognitive restructuring, journaling, and positive self-talk can promote positive thinking and improve emotional well-being.

Healthy Lifestyle Choices and Positive Thinking

A HEALTHY LIFESTYLE encompasses various aspects of daily living, including diet, exercise, sleep, and social interactions. Positive thinking can significantly influence these lifestyle choices, leading to better physical health outcomes.

1. Nutrition: A balanced diet is fundamental to physical health. Positive thinking can motivate individuals to make healthier food choices and maintain a nutritious diet. Instead of focusing on restrictive diets, approaching nutrition

with a positive mindset involves viewing food as nourishment and fuel for the body. Positive affirmations about self-worth and health can encourage better eating habits and reduce emotional eating.

2. Exercise: Regular physical activity is essential for maintaining physical health. Positive thinking can increase motivation and adherence to exercise routines. Viewing exercise as a rewarding and enjoyable activity, rather than a chore, can make it easier to incorporate into daily life. Positive self-talk and goal-setting can further enhance motivation and commitment to staying active.

3. Sleep: Quality sleep is crucial for overall health and well-being. Positive thinking can improve sleep by reducing stress and anxiety, which are common contributors to sleep disturbances. Establishing a positive bedtime routine, such as reading uplifting material, practicing gratitude, or engaging in relaxation techniques, can promote better sleep quality.

4. Social Connections: Building and nurturing positive relationships can enhance physical health. Social support can buffer against the negative effects of stress and promote a sense of belonging and purpose. Positive thinking can improve communication and foster healthier relationships, leading to better mental and physical health outcomes.

5. Avoiding Harmful Habits: Positive thinking can help individuals avoid harmful habits such as smoking, excessive alcohol consumption, and drug use. A positive mindset fosters a sense of self-worth and the desire to take care of one's body. Focusing on the benefits of a healthy lifestyle, rather than the restrictions, can make it easier to avoid these harmful behaviors.

6. Gratitude Practice: Practicing gratitude involves regularly reflecting on and appreciating the positive aspects of life. This practice has been shown to improve mental health and enhance overall well-being. Gratitude can shift focus away from negative thoughts and stressors, promoting a more positive outlook. By cultivating gratitude, individuals can foster a greater sense of contentment and improve their physical health.

7. Mind-Body Practices: Integrating mind-body practices such as yoga, tai chi, and qigong can promote physical health and positive thinking. These practices

combine physical movement with mindfulness and breath control, enhancing both physical and mental well-being. The emphasis on balance, flexibility, and relaxation in these practices can reduce stress and improve overall health.

Case Studies and Real-Life Examples

TO ILLUSTRATE THE PROFOUND impact of positive thinking on physical health, let's explore some real-life examples and case studies.

Case Study 1: Sarah's Journey to Wellness

SARAH, A 45-YEAR-OLD woman, had been struggling with chronic stress and its associated health problems for several years. She experienced frequent headaches, high blood pressure, and persistent fatigue. Sarah decided to adopt a more positive approach to life and incorporated various stress reduction techniques and healthy lifestyle choices into her daily routine.

Sarah started practicing mindfulness meditation for 20 minutes each morning. She found that this practice helped her manage stress and approach challenges with a more positive mindset. Additionally, she began engaging in regular physical activity, including yoga and daily walks in nature. These activities not only improved her physical fitness but also boosted her mood and energy levels.

To support her positive thinking journey, Sarah kept a gratitude journal, where she wrote down three things she was grateful for each day. This practice helped her focus on the positive aspects of her life and reduced her tendency to dwell on negative thoughts.

Over time, Sarah noticed significant improvements in her physical health. Her headaches became less frequent, her blood pressure stabilized, and she felt more energized and resilient. By embracing positive thinking and making healthier lifestyle choices, Sarah experienced a transformative improvement in her overall well-being.

Case Study 2: John's Battle with Chronic Pain

JOHN, A 50-YEAR-OLD man, had been living with chronic back pain for several years. The pain had a significant impact on his quality of life, leading to feelings of frustration and hopelessness. Despite trying various medical treatments, John's pain persisted, and he struggled to find relief.

John decided to explore alternative approaches to managing his pain and adopted a positive thinking mindset. He began practicing deep breathing exercises and progressive muscle relaxation to reduce tension and promote relaxation. John also incorporated positive affirmations into his daily routine, reminding himself of his strength and resilience.

In addition to these techniques, John started engaging in low-impact physical activities such as swimming and gentle stretching. These activities helped improve his physical fitness and reduce his pain levels. John also sought support from a chronic pain support group, where he connected with others facing similar challenges and gained valuable insights and encouragement.

As John continued to focus on positive thinking and healthy lifestyle choices, he noticed a gradual improvement in his pain levels and overall well-being. While his pain did not completely disappear, it became more manageable, and he regained a sense of control over his life. By embracing a positive mindset, John was able to improve his physical health and enhance his quality of life.

Case Study 3: Emma's Journey to Weight Loss

EMMA, A 35-YEAR-OLD woman, had struggled with her weight for most of her life. Despite numerous attempts to lose weight through restrictive diets and intense exercise programs, Emma found it challenging to achieve sustainable results. She often felt discouraged and experienced cycles of weight loss and gain.

Determined to make a lasting change, Emma decided to approach her weight loss journey with a positive mindset. Instead of focusing on what she couldn't eat, she began to view food as nourishment and made healthier choices that she enjoyed. Emma practiced positive self-talk, reminding herself of her worth and the importance of taking care of her body.

Emma also incorporated regular physical activity into her routine, choosing activities that she found enjoyable, such as dancing and hiking. She set realistic and achievable goals, celebrating her progress along the way. Emma joined a supportive community of individuals with similar goals, which provided her with motivation and encouragement.

Over time, Emma experienced significant improvements in her physical health. She lost weight gradually and sustainably, and her energy levels increased. Emma's positive mindset and healthy lifestyle choices not only helped her achieve her weight loss goals but also improved her overall well-being and self-esteem.

Scientific Evidence and Research

NUMEROUS SCIENTIFIC studies support the connection between positive thinking and physical health. Let's explore some of the key findings from this body of research.

1. Positive Thinking and Cardiovascular Health: A study published in the journal "Circulation" found that individuals with a positive outlook on life had a lower risk of developing cardiovascular disease. The researchers concluded that positive thinking could reduce stress, improve health behaviors, and enhance overall cardiovascular health.

2. Positive Thinking and Immune Function: Research published in "Psychological Science" demonstrated that positive emotions could boost immune function. The study found that individuals who experienced more positive emotions had higher levels of antibodies in response to a flu vaccine, suggesting a stronger immune response.

3. Positive Thinking and Longevity: A landmark study conducted by researchers at Yale University found that individuals with a positive attitude towards aging lived, on average, 7.5 years longer than those with a negative

attitude. The study highlighted the potential for positive thinking to influence longevity and overall health.

4. Positive Thinking and Pain Management: A review published in "Pain Medicine" examined the impact of positive thinking on pain management. The review concluded that positive thinking techniques, such as cognitive-behavioral therapy and positive self-talk, could significantly reduce pain perception and improve quality of life for individuals with chronic pain.

5. Positive Thinking and Mental Health: A study published in the "Journal of Positive Psychology" explored the relationship between positive thinking and mental health. The researchers found that individuals with a positive mindset were less likely to experience symptoms of depression and anxiety, and had better overall mental well-being.

Practical Tips for Cultivating Positive Thinking

CULTIVATING A POSITIVE mindset is a continuous process that requires intentional effort and practice. Here are some practical tips to help you develop and maintain positive thinking for better physical health:

1. Practice Gratitude: Take time each day to reflect on the things you are grateful for. Keeping a gratitude journal can help you focus on the positive aspects of your life and foster a sense of contentment.

2. Use Positive Affirmations: Incorporate positive affirmations into your daily routine. Repeat affirmations that resonate with you, such as "I am strong and capable," or "I choose to focus on the positive."

3. Surround Yourself with Positivity: Surround yourself with positive influences, including supportive friends, uplifting books, and motivational content. Avoid negative environments and people who bring you down.

4. Practice Mindfulness: Engage in mindfulness practices to stay present and cultivate a positive mindset. Mindfulness meditation, deep breathing exercises, and mindful eating can help you stay focused on the present moment.

5. Set Realistic Goals: Set achievable and realistic goals that align with your values and aspirations. Celebrate your progress and accomplishments, no matter how small.

6. Engage in Activities You Enjoy: Participate in activities that bring you joy and satisfaction. Engaging in hobbies and interests can boost your mood and foster a positive outlook.

7. Seek Support: Reach out for support when needed. Talking to a trusted friend, family member, or mental health professional can provide valuable perspective and encouragement.

8. Challenge Negative Thoughts: When negative thoughts arise, challenge them by examining the evidence and considering alternative perspectives. Replace negative thoughts with more positive and realistic ones.

9. Practice Self-Compassion: Be kind and compassionate towards yourself. Acknowledge your strengths and achievements, and forgive yourself for mistakes and setbacks.

10. Visualize Success: Use visualization techniques to imagine yourself achieving your goals and living a healthy, positive life. Visualization can enhance motivation and reinforce positive thinking.

Conclusion

The role of positive thinking in physical health is profound and multifaceted. The mind-body connection demonstrates how our thoughts and attitudes can influence our physiological responses and overall well-being. By incorporating stress reduction techniques and making healthy lifestyle choices, we can harness the power of positive thinking to enhance our physical health.

Real-life examples and scientific evidence underscore the significant impact that a positive mindset can have on various aspects of health, including cardiovascular function, immune response, pain management, and longevity. By cultivating positive thinking through practical strategies such as gratitude practice, positive affirmations, and mindfulness, we can improve our physical health and lead more fulfilling lives.

Remember, the journey to positive thinking is unique for each individual, and it requires ongoing effort and commitment. Embrace the process, be patient with yourself, and celebrate the positive changes that unfold. By nurturing a positive mindset, you can unlock the potential for better physical health and a more vibrant, joyful life.

Chapter 9: Positive Thinking in Relationships

Building Trust and Mutual Respect

Positive thinking plays a pivotal role in fostering trust and mutual respect in relationships. Trust is the cornerstone of any healthy relationship, whether it is romantic, familial, or platonic. It creates a safe environment where individuals feel secure, valued, and understood. Mutual respect further strengthens this foundation by ensuring that each person's feelings, opinions, and boundaries are acknowledged and honored.

The Role of Positive Thinking in Building Trust

Positive thinking can enhance trust in several ways. Firstly, it encourages individuals to see the best in their partners, focusing on their strengths and positive qualities rather than their flaws. This positive outlook fosters a sense of appreciation and gratitude, which can deepen the emotional bond between partners.

For example, consider a couple where one partner, Alex, tends to be forgetful. Instead of focusing on Alex's forgetfulness as a flaw, their partner, Jamie, chooses to highlight Alex's reliability and kindness in other areas. Jamie's positive thinking helps build trust by reinforcing Alex's positive attributes, which outweigh the occasional forgetfulness.

Positive thinking also promotes transparency and honesty, which are essential components of trust. When individuals approach their relationships with a positive mindset, they are more likely to communicate openly and honestly. They feel confident that their partners will respond with understanding and support, rather than judgment or criticism. This transparency nurtures a sense of security and trust within the relationship.

Mutual Respect through Positive Thinking

MUTUAL RESPECT INVOLVES recognizing and valuing each other's individuality, opinions, and boundaries. Positive thinking fosters mutual respect by encouraging partners to appreciate and celebrate their differences. Instead of viewing differences as obstacles, positive thinkers see them as opportunities for growth and learning.

For instance, in a relationship where one partner, Taylor, loves outdoor activities and the other, Jordan, prefers indoor hobbies, positive thinking can bridge the gap. Taylor and Jordan can choose to respect and support each other's interests, finding ways to enjoy both types of activities together. By valuing each other's preferences and making compromises, they build a relationship rooted in mutual respect.

Positive thinking also helps individuals to forgive and move past conflicts. Holding onto grudges and negative feelings can erode mutual respect. However, a positive mindset encourages forgiveness and understanding, allowing partners to resolve conflicts and rebuild respect. This approach strengthens the relationship, as both partners feel valued and understood.

Practical Steps to Foster Trust and Mutual Respect through Positive Thinking

1. PRACTICE GRATITUDE: Regularly express appreciation for your partner's positive qualities and actions. This practice reinforces positive thinking and strengthens trust.

2. Communicate Openly and Honestly: Share your thoughts, feelings, and concerns with your partner. Transparency builds trust and fosters a deeper emotional connection.

3. Respect Boundaries: Recognize and honor each other's personal boundaries. This respect demonstrates that you value your partner's individuality and autonomy.

4. Embrace Differences: Appreciate and celebrate the differences between you and your partner. View them as opportunities for growth rather than obstacles.

5. Forgive and Move On: Practice forgiveness and let go of grudges. Holding onto negative feelings can damage trust and mutual respect.

6. Support Each Other's Interests: Encourage and support your partner's interests and hobbies, even if they differ from your own. This support shows that you respect and value their individuality.

Effective Communication and Conflict Resolution

EFFECTIVE COMMUNICATION is the lifeblood of any healthy relationship. It allows partners to express their needs, desires, and concerns openly and honestly. Conflict is inevitable in any relationship, but how it is managed can either strengthen or weaken the bond between partners. Positive thinking plays a crucial role in both effective communication and conflict resolution.

The Role of Positive Thinking in Effective Communication

POSITIVE THINKING ENHANCES communication by promoting a constructive and empathetic approach. When individuals adopt a positive mindset, they are more likely to listen actively and empathetically. Active listening involves fully focusing on the speaker, understanding their message, and responding thoughtfully. This level of attentiveness fosters a deeper connection and mutual understanding.

For example, during a conversation about a sensitive topic, a positive thinker will approach the discussion with an open mind and a willingness to understand their partner's perspective. They will avoid interrupting, show genuine interest, and provide supportive feedback. This approach creates a safe space for open and honest communication.

Positive thinking also encourages the use of positive language. Positive language involves framing statements in a constructive and uplifting manner. Instead of focusing on what is wrong or criticizing their partner, positive thinkers highlight solutions and express their feelings in a respectful way.

Consider a scenario where one partner, Sam, feels neglected because the other partner, Casey, has been spending a lot of time at work. Instead of saying, "You never have time for me," Sam can use positive language: "I miss spending time with you and would love to plan some quality time together." This approach reduces defensiveness and opens the door for a constructive conversation.

Conflict Resolution through Positive Thinking

CONFLICT IS A NATURAL part of any relationship, but it does not have to be destructive. Positive thinking can transform conflicts into opportunities for growth and deeper understanding. When approached with a positive mindset, conflicts can be resolved in a way that strengthens the relationship.

Positive thinkers approach conflicts with a solution-oriented mindset. Instead of dwelling on the problem or assigning blame, they focus on finding mutually beneficial solutions. This approach fosters collaboration and cooperation, rather than competition and hostility.

For instance, if partners are arguing about household chores, a positive thinker will focus on finding a fair and practical solution. They might suggest creating a chore schedule or dividing tasks based on each partner's strengths and preferences. This collaborative approach reduces tension and promotes harmony.

Positive thinking also encourages empathy and understanding during conflicts. Empathy involves putting oneself in the other person's shoes and trying to understand their feelings and perspective. By practicing empathy, positive thinkers can respond to conflicts with compassion and respect.

During a disagreement, a positive thinker might say, "I understand that you're feeling stressed about work, and I appreciate how hard you're working. Let's find a way to manage this together." This empathetic response shows understanding and support, which can de-escalate the conflict and pave the way for resolution.

Practical Steps for Effective Communication and Conflict Resolution through Positive Thinking

1. LISTEN ACTIVELY and Empathetically: Focus fully on your partner during conversations. Show genuine interest and empathy for their perspective.

2. Use Positive Language: Frame your statements in a constructive and respectful manner. Highlight solutions and express your feelings positively.

3. Stay Solution-Oriented: Focus on finding mutually beneficial solutions during conflicts. Avoid dwelling on the problem or assigning blame.

4. Practice Empathy: Put yourself in your partner's shoes and try to understand their feelings and perspective. Respond with compassion and respect.

5. Manage Emotions: Stay calm and composed during conflicts. Avoid letting negative emotions escalate the situation.

6. Set Boundaries: Establish clear and respectful boundaries for communication and conflict resolution. Ensure that both partners feel heard and respected.

7. Seek Compromise: Be willing to compromise and find middle ground. Flexibility and willingness to meet halfway can resolve conflicts amicably.

8. Reflect and Learn: After resolving a conflict, take time to reflect on what you have learned. Use this insight to improve future communication and conflict resolution.

Supporting and Encouraging Loved Ones

SUPPORTING AND ENCOURAGING loved ones is an essential aspect of any meaningful relationship. Positive thinking can significantly enhance the way we provide support and encouragement, creating a nurturing and empowering environment for our partners, family members, and friends.

The Role of Positive Thinking in Providing Support

POSITIVE THINKING ENABLES individuals to offer support in a compassionate and uplifting manner. When we approach our relationships with a positive mindset, we are more likely to provide emotional and practical support that genuinely benefits our loved ones.

Emotional Support through Positive Thinking

EMOTIONAL SUPPORT INVOLVES offering empathy, understanding, and encouragement. Positive thinkers are adept at providing emotional support because they focus on uplifting and reassuring their loved ones. They validate their partner's feelings and experiences, creating a sense of emotional safety and security.

For example, if a loved one is going through a difficult time at work, a positive thinker might say, "I know this situation is challenging, but I believe in your ability to overcome it. You're strong and capable, and I'm here for you every step of the way." This type of encouragement fosters resilience and confidence in the face of adversity.

Positive thinkers also use active listening to provide emotional support. They give their full attention to their loved ones, allowing them to express their feelings without judgment or interruption. This level of attentiveness shows that they genuinely care and are invested in their partner's well-being.

Practical Support through Positive Thinking

PRACTICAL SUPPORT INVOLVES offering tangible assistance to help loved ones navigate challenges and achieve their goals. Positive thinkers are proactive in identifying ways to help and provide support in a constructive manner.

For instance, if a family member is struggling to balance work and personal responsibilities, a positive thinker might offer to help with specific tasks, such as running errands or preparing meals. They approach the situation with a positive attitude, focusing on how they can make a difference and alleviate stress.

Positive thinkers also encourage their loved ones to pursue their dreams and aspirations. They provide motivation and inspiration, helping their partners stay focused and driven. By celebrating their achievements and offering positive reinforcement, they create an environment where their loved ones feel supported and valued.

Encouraging Loved Ones through Positive Thinking

ENCOURAGEMENT IS A powerful tool that can boost confidence, motivation, and overall well-being. Positive thinking enhances the way we encourage our loved ones, making our support more impactful and meaningful.

Building Confidence through Positive Reinforcement

POSITIVE THINKERS USE positive reinforcement to build their loved ones' confidence. They acknowledge and celebrate their partner's achievements, no matter how small, and provide genuine praise and encouragement.

For example, if a friend is working towards a personal goal, a positive thinker might say, "I'm so proud of the progress you've made. Your dedication and hard work are truly inspiring. Keep going, and you'll achieve amazing things." This type of encouragement reinforces their friend's self-belief and determination.

Positive thinkers also help their loved ones reframe setbacks and challenges. Instead of focusing on failures, they emphasize the lessons learned and the potential for growth. This positive perspective encourages resilience and a growth mindset.

Motivating Loved Ones through Positive Affirmations

POSITIVE AFFIRMATIONS are powerful statements that reinforce self-belief and motivation. Positive thinkers use affirmations to uplift and inspire their loved ones, helping them stay focused and driven.

For instance, if a partner is feeling discouraged about a challenging project, a positive thinker might say, "You have the skills and talent to succeed. I believe in you, and I know you can do this. Stay positive and keep pushing forward." These affirmations provide a motivational boost and remind their partner of their capabilities.

Positive thinkers also encourage their loved ones to set realistic and achievable goals. They provide guidance and support in creating actionable plans, helping their partners stay on track and motivated.

Practical Steps for Supporting and Encouraging Loved Ones through Positive Thinking

1. OFFER EMPATHY AND Understanding: Validate your loved one's feelings and experiences. Show empathy and understanding to create emotional safety.

2. Use Positive Language: Frame your support and encouragement in a positive and uplifting manner. Highlight their strengths and potential.

3. Provide Active Listening: Give your full attention to your loved ones. Listen actively and respond thoughtfully to their needs and concerns.

4. Offer Practical Assistance: Identify specific ways to help and provide tangible support. Approach the situation with a positive attitude and focus on making a difference.

5. Celebrate Achievements: Acknowledge and celebrate your loved one's accomplishments. Provide genuine praise and encouragement to build their confidence.

6. Reframe Setbacks: Help your loved ones reframe setbacks and challenges as opportunities for growth. Emphasize the lessons learned and potential for improvement.

7. Use Positive Affirmations: Provide positive affirmations to uplift and inspire your loved ones. Reinforce their self-belief and motivation.

8. Encourage Goal Setting: Support your loved ones in setting realistic and achievable goals. Provide guidance and encouragement to help them stay focused and driven.

9. Be Present and Available: Make time for your loved ones and be present in their lives. Show that you care by being there for them during both good times and challenges.

10. Practice Patience and Understanding: Understand that everyone has their own pace and journey. Be patient and offer consistent support, even during difficult times.

Case Studies and Real-Life Examples

TO ILLUSTRATE THE PROFOUND impact of positive thinking on relationships, let's explore some real-life examples and case studies.

Case Study 1: Emily and David's Journey to Trust and Mutual Respect

EMILY AND DAVID HAD been married for five years, but their relationship was strained due to frequent misunderstandings and conflicts. They realized that their lack of trust and mutual respect was taking a toll on their marriage and decided to seek help.

With the guidance of a therapist, Emily and David learned to incorporate positive thinking into their relationship. They started practicing gratitude by regularly expressing appreciation for each other's positive qualities and actions. This practice helped them shift their focus from their partner's flaws to their strengths, fostering a sense of gratitude and trust.

Emily and David also worked on improving their communication. They learned to listen actively and empathetically, allowing each other to express their thoughts and feelings without judgment. They used positive language to frame their statements constructively, which reduced defensiveness and facilitated open discussions.

As they continued to embrace positive thinking, Emily and David noticed significant improvements in their relationship. They rebuilt trust and mutual respect, and their conflicts became less frequent and more manageable. Their marriage grew stronger, and they felt more connected and supported.

Case Study 2: Sarah and Mark's Effective Communication and Conflict Resolution

SARAH AND MARK WERE in a long-term relationship but struggled with effective communication and conflict resolution. Their arguments often escalated into heated exchanges, leaving both feeling hurt and misunderstood.

Determined to improve their relationship, Sarah and Mark decided to adopt a positive thinking approach. They started by practicing active listening and empathy during their conversations. They made a conscious effort to fully focus on each other, understand each other's perspectives, and respond with compassion.

Sarah and Mark also began using positive language to express their feelings and needs. Instead of blaming or criticizing, they focused on finding solutions and expressing their emotions constructively. This shift in communication style reduced tension and created a more supportive environment.

When conflicts arose, Sarah and Mark approached them with a solution-oriented mindset. They collaborated to find mutually beneficial solutions and practiced empathy to understand each other's feelings. By staying calm and composed, they were able to resolve conflicts amicably.

As they continued to incorporate positive thinking into their communication and conflict resolution, Sarah and Mark experienced significant improvements in their relationship. They felt more understood and supported, and their conflicts became opportunities for growth and deeper connection.

Case Study 3: Jennifer and Paul's Journey of Support and Encouragement

JENNIFER AND PAUL HAD been friends for over a decade. Jennifer was going through a challenging time, dealing with job loss and personal setbacks. Paul, a positive thinker, decided to offer his support and encouragement to help Jennifer navigate this difficult period.

Paul provided emotional support by listening actively and empathetically to Jennifer's concerns. He validated her feelings and offered words of encouragement, reminding her of her strengths and resilience. Paul also used positive affirmations to uplift Jennifer, reinforcing her self-belief and motivation.

In addition to emotional support, Paul offered practical assistance. He helped Jennifer update her resume, prepared her for job interviews, and provided resources for career development. Paul's proactive approach and positive attitude made a significant difference in Jennifer's confidence and outlook.

As Jennifer began to rebuild her life, she felt grateful for Paul's unwavering support and encouragement. She regained her confidence, secured a new job, and felt more empowered to pursue her goals. Paul's positive thinking and support played a crucial role in Jennifer's journey to recovery and success.

Scientific Evidence and Research

NUMEROUS SCIENTIFIC studies support the connection between positive thinking and relationship quality. Let's explore some of the key findings from this body of research.

1. Positive Thinking and Relationship Satisfaction: A study published in the "Journal of Personality and Social Psychology" found that individuals with a positive outlook on life reported higher levels of relationship satisfaction. Positive thinking was associated with better communication, increased trust, and greater mutual respect.

2. Positive Thinking and Conflict Resolution: Research published in "Personal Relationships" demonstrated that positive thinking could improve conflict resolution in romantic relationships. Couples who adopted a positive mindset were more likely to approach conflicts collaboratively and find mutually beneficial solutions.

3. Positive Thinking and Emotional Support: A study published in the "Journal of Social and Personal Relationships" explored the impact of positive thinking on emotional support. The researchers found that individuals with a positive outlook were more effective at providing empathetic and uplifting support to their partners.

4. Positive Thinking and Marital Quality: Research published in "Psychological Science" examined the role of positive thinking in marital quality. The study concluded that couples who practiced positive thinking and gratitude experienced higher levels of marital satisfaction and stability.

5. Positive Thinking and Well-Being: A study published in the "Journal of Positive Psychology" explored the relationship between positive thinking and overall well-being. The researchers found that individuals who practiced positive thinking experienced better mental and emotional health, which positively influenced their relationships.

Practical Tips for Cultivating Positive Thinking in Relationships

CULTIVATING POSITIVE thinking in relationships requires intentional effort and practice. Here are some practical tips to help you develop and maintain positive thinking for better relationship quality:

1. Practice Gratitude: Regularly express appreciation for your partner's positive qualities and actions. This practice reinforces positive thinking and strengthens trust and mutual respect.

2. Use Positive Language: Frame your communication in a constructive and respectful manner. Highlight solutions and express your feelings positively to reduce defensiveness and promote understanding.

3. Listen Actively and Empathetically: Focus fully on your partner during conversations. Show genuine interest and empathy for their perspective to foster deeper connection and mutual understanding.

4. Stay Solution-Oriented: Approach conflicts with a solution-oriented mindset. Focus on finding mutually beneficial solutions rather than dwelling on the problem or assigning blame.

5. Provide Emotional Support: Offer empathy, understanding, and encouragement to your loved ones. Validate their feelings and experiences to create emotional safety and security.

6. Offer Practical Assistance: Identify specific ways to help and provide tangible support to your loved ones. Approach the situation with a positive attitude and focus on making a difference.

7. Celebrate Achievements: Acknowledge and celebrate your loved one's accomplishments. Provide genuine praise and encouragement to build their confidence and motivation.

8. Reframe Setbacks: Help your loved ones reframe setbacks and challenges as opportunities for growth. Emphasize the lessons learned and potential for improvement.

9. Use Positive Affirmations: Provide positive affirmations to uplift and inspire your loved ones. Reinforce their self-belief and motivation to help them stay focused and driven.

10. Encourage Goal Setting: Support your loved ones in setting realistic and achievable goals. Provide guidance and encouragement to help them stay focused and motivated.

11. Be Present and Available: Make time for your loved ones and be present in their lives. Show that you care by being there for them during both good times and challenges.

12. Practice Patience and Understanding: Understand that everyone has their own pace and journey. Be patient and offer consistent support, even during difficult times.

Conclusion

POSITIVE THINKING HAS a profound impact on relationships, enhancing trust, mutual respect, effective communication, conflict resolution, and support and encouragement. By cultivating a positive mindset, individuals can foster deeper connections, stronger bonds, and more fulfilling relationships.

Building trust and mutual respect through positive thinking involves focusing on each other's strengths, practicing gratitude, and approaching differences as opportunities for growth. Effective communication and conflict resolution are enhanced by active listening, positive language, empathy, and a solution-oriented mindset.

Supporting and encouraging loved ones through positive thinking involves offering empathy, practical assistance, and positive affirmations. By creating a nurturing and empowering environment, positive thinkers help their partners, family members, and friends achieve their goals and navigate challenges with confidence.

Scientific evidence supports the connection between positive thinking and relationship quality, highlighting the benefits of a positive outlook on trust, communication, conflict resolution, and overall well-being. By incorporating practical strategies for positive thinking, individuals can improve their relationship quality and lead more meaningful and fulfilling lives.

Remember, the journey to positive thinking in relationships is unique for each individual and requires ongoing effort and commitment. Embrace the process, be patient with yourself and your loved ones, and celebrate the positive changes that unfold. By nurturing a positive mindset, you can unlock the potential for stronger, healthier, and more satisfying relationships.

Chapter 10: Positive Thinking for Personal Growth

Setting and Achieving Goals

Setting and achieving goals is a foundational aspect of personal growth, and positive thinking plays a crucial role in this process. Goals give our lives direction, provide a sense of purpose, and motivate us to push beyond our comfort zones. Positive thinking helps to transform these aspirations into achievable realities by fostering a mindset of possibility, resilience, and determination.

The Importance of Goal Setting**

GOAL SETTING IS VITAL for several reasons. Firstly, it provides clarity. When we set specific goals, we create a clear vision of what we want to achieve. This clarity helps to focus our efforts and resources on activities that will bring us closer to our objectives.

Secondly, goals provide motivation. They act as a source of inspiration and energy, driving us to take action. The anticipation of achieving a goal can boost our enthusiasm and keep us motivated even when faced with challenges.

Lastly, setting and achieving goals fosters a sense of accomplishment and boosts self-confidence. Each goal achieved is a testament to our abilities and effort, reinforcing our belief in ourselves and our potential.

The Role of Positive Thinking in Goal Setting

POSITIVE THINKING IS essential in goal setting as it influences our mindset and approach. A positive mindset encourages us to set ambitious goals, believe in our abilities, and maintain perseverance in the face of setbacks.

1. Believing in Possibilities: Positive thinkers believe that they can achieve their goals. This belief in possibility is crucial for setting ambitious and meaningful goals. When we approach goal setting with a positive mindset, we are more likely to aim high and pursue our dreams with confidence.

2. Visualizing Success: Visualization is a powerful tool for achieving goals. Positive thinkers use visualization techniques to imagine themselves achieving their goals. This mental imagery reinforces their commitment and motivation, making the goals feel more attainable.

3. Maintaining Resilience: The path to achieving goals is often fraught with challenges and setbacks. Positive thinking fosters resilience, enabling individuals to bounce back from failures and keep moving forward. Instead of giving up when faced with obstacles, positive thinkers see these challenges as opportunities for growth and learning.

Steps for Effective Goal Setting and Achievement

1. DEFINE CLEAR AND Specific Goals: Goals should be clear, specific, and measurable. Instead of setting a vague goal like "get fit," define a specific objective such as "run a 5k race in three months." Specific goals provide a clear target and make it easier to track progress.

2. Set Realistic and Achievable Goals: While it's important to aim high, goals should also be realistic and achievable. Setting unattainable goals can lead to frustration and discouragement. Break down larger goals into smaller, manageable steps to make them more achievable.

3. Create a Detailed Action Plan: Develop a detailed action plan outlining the steps needed to achieve your goals. This plan should include specific tasks, deadlines, and milestones. Having a clear plan of action helps to maintain focus and momentum.

4. Stay Committed and Motivated: Maintain a strong commitment to your goals by regularly reminding yourself of why they are important. Use positive affirmations, visualization, and motivational quotes to stay inspired and focused.

5. Track Progress and Adjust as Needed: Regularly track your progress towards your goals. Celebrate small victories along the way to maintain motivation. Be flexible and willing to adjust your action plan if necessary. Positive thinkers understand that setbacks are part of the journey and use them as learning experiences.

6. Seek Support and Accountability: Share your goals with supportive friends, family members, or mentors who can provide encouragement and hold you accountable. Joining a community or group with similar goals can also provide valuable support and motivation.

Case Study: Anna's Journey to Starting Her Own Business

ANNA HAD ALWAYS DREAMED of starting her own business, but she was unsure of where to begin. She decided to adopt a positive thinking approach to goal setting and achievement.

Anna began by defining her goal: to launch an online boutique selling handmade jewelry within six months. She broke this goal down into smaller, manageable steps, such as researching the market, creating a business plan, designing her products, and setting up an e-commerce website.

Anna used visualization techniques to imagine herself successfully running her boutique. She created a vision board with images representing her goals and placed it in her workspace as a daily reminder of her aspirations.

To stay motivated, Anna practiced positive affirmations and regularly reminded herself of her strengths and capabilities. She sought support from a local business group, where she connected with other aspiring entrepreneurs who provided encouragement and advice.

Despite facing challenges along the way, such as finding suppliers and managing her time, Anna remained resilient. She viewed each setback as a learning opportunity and adjusted her action plan as needed.

Six months later, Anna successfully launched her online boutique. Her positive thinking approach played a crucial role in setting and achieving her goal, and she felt a profound sense of accomplishment and confidence in her abilities.

Embracing Change and Uncertainty

CHANGE AND UNCERTAINTY are inevitable aspects of life. While they can be daunting, they also present opportunities for growth, learning, and transformation. Positive thinking equips us with the mindset and tools to embrace change and navigate uncertainty with confidence and resilience.

The Nature of Change and Uncertainty

CHANGE CAN TAKE MANY forms, including personal transitions, career shifts, relationship changes, and societal developments. Uncertainty often accompanies change, as it involves stepping into the unknown and facing unpredictable outcomes.

Many people find change and uncertainty challenging because they disrupt familiar routines and create a sense of instability. However, how we perceive and respond to change can significantly impact our experience and outcomes.

The Role of Positive Thinking in Embracing Change

POSITIVE THINKING HELPS individuals embrace change by fostering a mindset of openness, adaptability, and optimism. It encourages us to view change as an opportunity for growth rather than a threat.

1. Cultivating an Open Mindset: Positive thinkers approach change with an open mind. They are willing to explore new possibilities, adapt to new circumstances, and embrace different perspectives. This openness allows them to navigate change more effectively and seize opportunities for growth.

2. Building Adaptability and Resilience: Positive thinking enhances our adaptability and resilience. Positive thinkers are more likely to see challenges as temporary and solvable. They are better equipped to bounce back from setbacks, learn from experiences, and adjust their strategies as needed.

3. Maintaining Optimism and Hope: Optimism is a key component of positive thinking. Optimistic individuals believe that positive outcomes are possible, even in the face of uncertainty. This hopeful outlook helps them stay motivated and focused on their goals, despite the challenges that change may bring.

Strategies for Embracing Change and Uncertainty

1. ACCEPT AND ACKNOWLEDGE Change: The first step in embracing change is to accept and acknowledge it. Denying or resisting change can lead to unnecessary stress and frustration. Accepting change allows us to move forward with a proactive and positive mindset.

2. Focus on What You Can Control: During times of change and uncertainty, it is essential to focus on what you can control. Identify the aspects of the situation that you can influence and take positive actions in those areas. This focus helps to reduce feelings of helplessness and empowers you to make meaningful progress.

3. Develop a Growth Mindset: A growth mindset involves viewing challenges and setbacks as opportunities for learning and growth. Embrace change with a curiosity-driven approach, seeking to learn new skills, gain new experiences, and expand your horizons.

4. Practice Self-Compassion: Be kind and compassionate towards yourself during times of change. Understand that it is normal to feel uncertain or anxious, and give yourself permission to experience these emotions without judgment. Self-compassion helps to build resilience and maintain a positive outlook.

5. Seek Support and Connection: Reach out to supportive friends, family members, or mentors who can provide guidance and encouragement. Sharing your experiences and feelings with others can help to alleviate stress and provide valuable perspectives.

6. Stay Flexible and Adaptable: Flexibility is key to navigating change successfully. Be willing to adjust your plans and strategies as needed. Stay open to new opportunities and be prepared to pivot when necessary.

7. Visualize Positive Outcomes: Use visualization techniques to imagine positive outcomes and scenarios. This mental imagery can help to reinforce your optimism and motivation, making it easier to embrace change with confidence.

Case Study: Michael's Career Transition

MICHAEL HAD BEEN WORKING in the same industry for over a decade when he was unexpectedly laid off due to company downsizing. Initially, he felt a sense of uncertainty and fear about his future. However, he decided to adopt a positive thinking approach to embrace this career transition.

Michael began by accepting and acknowledging the change. He recognized that losing his job was beyond his control, but he could control how he responded to it. He focused on the aspects he could influence, such as updating his resume, networking, and exploring new career opportunities.

Michael developed a growth mindset by viewing this transition as an opportunity to learn and grow. He enrolled in online courses to acquire new skills and expand his knowledge. He also attended industry conferences and workshops to stay updated on the latest trends and connect with professionals in his field.

Throughout this process, Michael practiced self-compassion. He acknowledged his feelings of uncertainty and allowed himself to experience them without judgment. He also sought support from his family and friends, who provided encouragement and valuable advice.

Michael stayed flexible and adaptable, being open to exploring different career paths. He visualized positive outcomes, imagining himself thriving in a new role that aligned with his passions and strengths.

Eventually, Michael secured a new job in a different industry that offered better opportunities for growth and advancement. His positive thinking approach played a crucial role in navigating this career transition and embracing change with confidence and resilience.

Lifelong Learning and Self-Improvement

LIFELONG LEARNING AND self-improvement are essential components of personal growth. They involve a continuous commitment to acquiring new knowledge, developing skills, and enhancing one's overall well-being. Positive thinking fuels this journey by fostering a mindset of curiosity, motivation, and self-belief.

The Importance of Lifelong Learning and Self-Improvement

LIFELONG LEARNING AND self-improvement have numerous benefits. They help individuals stay intellectually engaged, adapt to changing circumstances, and achieve personal and professional growth. By continuously seeking to improve, individuals can enhance their quality of life, build resilience, and achieve their full potential.

1. Staying Intellectually Engaged: Lifelong learning keeps the mind active and engaged. It helps to prevent cognitive decline and promotes mental agility. Engaging in learning activities such as reading, taking courses, or pursuing hobbies stimulates the brain and fosters intellectual growth.

2. Adapting to Change: In a rapidly changing world, the ability to learn and adapt is crucial. Lifelong learning equips individuals with the skills and knowledge needed to navigate new challenges and seize emerging opportunities. It enhances adaptability and ensures that individuals remain relevant and competitive.

3. Achieving Personal and Professional Growth: Self-improvement is key to achieving personal and professional goals. By continuously seeking to improve, individuals can enhance their skills, build confidence, and achieve greater success in their careers and personal lives.

The Role of Positive Thinking in Lifelong Learning and Self-Improvement

POSITIVE THINKING ENHANCES lifelong learning and self-improvement by fostering a mindset of curiosity, motivation, and self-belief. It encourages individuals to embrace challenges, seek new experiences, and continuously strive for growth.

1. Cultivating Curiosity and a Love for Learning: Positive thinkers have a natural curiosity and a love for learning. They approach new knowledge and experiences with enthusiasm and a desire to grow. This curiosity drives them to explore new subjects, ask questions, and seek out opportunities for learning.

2. Staying Motivated and Focused: Positive thinking helps individuals stay motivated and focused on their learning and self-improvement goals. Positive affirmations, visualization, and goal-setting techniques can reinforce motivation and keep individuals committed to their growth journey.

3. Building Self-Belief and Confidence: Positive thinkers believe in their abilities and potential. This self-belief is crucial for lifelong learning and self-improvement, as it empowers individuals to take on new challenges, overcome obstacles, and achieve their goals.

Strategies for Lifelong Learning and Self-Improvement

1. SET LEARNING GOALS: Define clear and specific learning goals. Identify the areas you want to improve and the skills you want to acquire. Setting goals provides direction and motivation for your learning journey.

2. Develop a Learning Plan: Create a detailed learning plan outlining the steps needed to achieve your goals. Include specific tasks, resources, and deadlines. A well-structured plan helps to maintain focus and momentum.

3. Embrace a Growth Mindset: Adopt a growth mindset by viewing challenges and setbacks as opportunities for learning and growth. Approach new experiences with curiosity and a willingness to learn.

4. Seek Out Learning Opportunities: Actively seek out learning opportunities such as courses, workshops, seminars, books, and online resources. Engage in activities that stimulate your mind and foster intellectual growth.

5. Practice Self-Reflection: Regularly reflect on your learning experiences and progress. Identify areas for improvement and celebrate your achievements. Self-reflection helps to reinforce positive thinking and maintain motivation.

6. Stay Open to Feedback: Be open to feedback from others. Constructive feedback provides valuable insights and helps to identify areas for improvement. Use feedback as a tool for growth and self-improvement.

7. Create a Supportive Environment: Surround yourself with supportive individuals who encourage your learning and growth. Join learning communities or groups with similar interests to share knowledge and experiences.

8. Stay Flexible and Adaptable: Be willing to adjust your learning plan and goals as needed. Stay open to new opportunities and be prepared to pivot when necessary.

Case Study: Rachel's Journey of Lifelong Learning

RACHEL HAD ALWAYS BEEN passionate about learning, but her busy career and personal life left little time for self-improvement. Determined to prioritize lifelong learning, she adopted a positive thinking approach to achieve her learning goals.

Rachel began by setting clear learning goals. She identified areas she wanted to improve, such as leadership skills, digital marketing, and personal wellness. She developed a detailed learning plan that included specific tasks, resources, and deadlines for each goal.

To stay motivated, Rachel practiced positive affirmations and visualization. She imagined herself successfully acquiring new skills and achieving her goals. She also sought out learning opportunities, such as enrolling in online courses, attending workshops, and reading books on her chosen subjects.

Rachel embraced a growth mindset by viewing challenges as opportunities for learning. When faced with setbacks, she reminded herself that these experiences were valuable for her growth. She practiced self-reflection regularly, assessing her progress and identifying areas for improvement.

Throughout her journey, Rachel stayed open to feedback from mentors and peers. She used their insights to refine her learning strategies and make meaningful progress. She also created a supportive environment by joining learning communities and connecting with like-minded individuals.

As Rachel continued her lifelong learning journey, she experienced significant personal and professional growth. She developed new skills, enhanced her knowledge, and improved her overall well-being. Her positive thinking approach played a crucial role in her success, empowering her to embrace lifelong learning and achieve her full potential.

Conclusion

Positive thinking is a powerful tool for personal growth, influencing our ability to set and achieve goals, embrace change and uncertainty, and pursue lifelong learning and self-improvement. By fostering a mindset of possibility, resilience, and motivation, positive thinking enables us to navigate life's challenges and achieve our aspirations.

Setting and achieving goals with a positive mindset involves believing in possibilities, visualizing success, maintaining resilience, and creating a detailed action plan. Embracing change and uncertainty requires an open mindset, adaptability, optimism, and a focus on what we can control. Lifelong learning and self-improvement are driven by curiosity, motivation, self-belief, and a commitment to continuous growth.

By incorporating practical strategies for positive thinking, individuals can enhance their personal growth journey and achieve greater success and fulfillment. Remember, the journey to personal growth is unique for each individual and requires ongoing effort and commitment. Embrace the process, be patient with yourself, and celebrate the positive changes that unfold. By nurturing a positive mindset, you can unlock the potential for a more meaningful and fulfilling life.

Chapter 11: Positive Thinking in the Workplace

Enhancing Productivity and Creativity

Positive thinking is a powerful catalyst for enhancing productivity and creativity in the workplace. It influences how employees approach their tasks, interact with colleagues, and handle challenges, ultimately shaping the overall work environment and organizational success.

The Role of Positive Thinking in Productivity

PRODUCTIVITY IS THE efficiency with which tasks and goals are accomplished. Positive thinking boosts productivity by fostering motivation, focus, and resilience. When employees maintain a positive mindset, they are more likely to stay engaged, overcome obstacles, and consistently perform at their best.

1. Motivation and Engagement: Positive thinking fuels intrinsic motivation, which is the inner drive to pursue goals and complete tasks. Motivated employees are more engaged in their work, taking initiative and putting in the effort needed to achieve high-quality results. They view their work as meaningful and are more committed to contributing to the organization's success.

2. Focus and Concentration: A positive mindset enhances focus and concentration. When employees approach their tasks with optimism, they are less likely to be distracted by negative thoughts or external stressors. This heightened focus allows them to work more efficiently and produce higher-quality output.

3. Resilience and Problem-Solving: Positive thinking equips employees with the resilience to handle setbacks and challenges. Instead of becoming discouraged by obstacles, they view them as opportunities for growth and

learning. This problem-solving mindset enables them to find innovative solutions and maintain productivity even in difficult situations.

Strategies for Enhancing Productivity through Positive Thinking

1. SET CLEAR GOALS and Priorities: Clearly defined goals and priorities provide a sense of direction and purpose. Encourage employees to set specific, achievable goals and prioritize their tasks accordingly. Positive thinking can help them stay focused and motivated to achieve these goals.

2. Foster a Positive Work Environment: Create a supportive and positive work environment where employees feel valued and appreciated. Recognize and celebrate their achievements, provide constructive feedback, and encourage open communication. A positive work environment boosts morale and enhances productivity.

3. Encourage Breaks and Downtime: Regular breaks and downtime are essential for maintaining productivity. Encourage employees to take short breaks to recharge and prevent burnout. Positive thinking can help them view breaks as opportunities to rejuvenate and return to their tasks with renewed energy.

4. Promote Work-Life Balance: Support employees in achieving a healthy work-life balance. Flexible work arrangements, wellness programs, and promoting time management skills can help them manage their work responsibilities while maintaining their overall well-being. Positive thinking reinforces the importance of balance and self-care.

5. Provide Opportunities for Growth and Development: Invest in employee development by offering training, workshops, and opportunities for skill enhancement. Positive thinking encourages employees to view learning as a continuous process and motivates them to seek out growth opportunities.

The Role of Positive Thinking in Creativity

CREATIVITY IS THE ABILITY to generate new and innovative ideas. Positive thinking nurtures creativity by fostering an open and exploratory mindset, reducing fear of failure, and encouraging risk-taking.

1. Open and Exploratory Mindset: Positive thinking encourages an open and exploratory mindset, where employees are willing to experiment with new ideas and approaches. This openness leads to a greater diversity of thought and more innovative solutions.

2. Reduced Fear of Failure: Fear of failure can stifle creativity. Positive thinking helps to reduce this fear by promoting a growth mindset, where mistakes are viewed as learning opportunities. Employees are more likely to take risks and think outside the box when they are not afraid of failure.

3. Encouraging Risk-Taking: Creativity often involves taking risks and challenging the status quo. Positive thinking empowers employees to take calculated risks and explore unconventional ideas. This risk-taking is essential for driving innovation and staying competitive in a dynamic business environment.

Strategies for Enhancing Creativity through Positive Thinking

1. ENCOURAGE BRAINSTORMING and Collaboration: Create opportunities for brainstorming and collaboration. Encourage employees to share their ideas freely and build on each other's contributions. Positive thinking fosters a collaborative atmosphere where creativity can thrive.

2. Provide a Safe Space for Experimentation: Establish a safe space for experimentation, where employees can test new ideas without fear of negative consequences. Encourage a culture of experimentation and innovation, where failures are seen as part of the learning process.

3. Offer Creative Freedom and Autonomy: Give employees the autonomy to explore their ideas and approaches. Trusting them with creative freedom fosters

a sense of ownership and responsibility, which can lead to more innovative solutions.

4. Promote Diverse Perspectives: Diversity of thought is crucial for creativity. Encourage a diverse and inclusive work environment where different perspectives are valued and considered. Positive thinking helps to appreciate and leverage this diversity for creative problem-solving.

5. Celebrate Creativity and Innovation: Recognize and celebrate creativity and innovation within the organization. Highlight successful projects and initiatives that resulted from creative thinking. Positive reinforcement boosts confidence and motivates employees to continue thinking creatively.

Case Study: Enhancing Productivity and Creativity at InnovateTech

INNOVATETECH, A TECHNOLOGY company, wanted to enhance productivity and creativity among its employees. The company decided to implement a positive thinking approach to achieve these goals.

InnovateTech started by setting clear goals and priorities for its teams. Managers worked with employees to define specific, achievable objectives and create detailed action plans. This clarity provided a sense of direction and motivation.

The company also focused on creating a positive work environment. Managers recognized and celebrated employees' achievements through regular appreciation events and feedback sessions. Open communication was encouraged, and employees felt valued and supported.

To prevent burnout, InnovateTech promoted regular breaks and downtime. Employees were encouraged to take short breaks throughout the day and participate in wellness programs. The company also supported work-life balance through flexible work arrangements and time management workshops.

InnovateTech invested in employee development by offering training and workshops on new technologies and skills. Positive thinking encouraged employees to view learning as a continuous process, and they actively sought out growth opportunities.

To enhance creativity, InnovateTech encouraged brainstorming and collaboration. Teams held regular brainstorming sessions where employees could share their ideas freely. The company established a safe space for experimentation, where employees could test new concepts without fear of failure.

InnovateTech also promoted creative freedom and autonomy. Employees were trusted with the autonomy to explore their ideas and approaches. The company valued diverse perspectives and encouraged a diverse and inclusive work environment.

As a result of these initiatives, InnovateTech saw a significant increase in productivity and creativity. Employees were more engaged, motivated, and innovative. The positive thinking approach played a crucial role in creating a thriving and dynamic work environment.

Building Positive Work Relationships

POSITIVE WORK RELATIONSHIPS are essential for a healthy and productive workplace. They foster collaboration, improve communication, and enhance overall job satisfaction. Positive thinking is a key factor in building and maintaining these relationships, as it promotes empathy, respect, and effective communication.

The Importance of Positive Work Relationships

POSITIVE WORK RELATIONSHIPS have numerous benefits. They improve teamwork and collaboration, leading to more efficient and effective problem-solving. They also enhance employee morale and job satisfaction, reducing turnover and absenteeism. Positive relationships create a supportive work environment where employees feel valued and motivated.

The Role of Positive Thinking in Building Work Relationships

POSITIVE THINKING ENHANCES work relationships by fostering empathy, respect, and effective communication. It encourages employees to approach interactions with a positive and open mindset, creating a harmonious and supportive work environment.

1. Empathy and Understanding: Positive thinking promotes empathy and understanding. Empathetic employees are better able to relate to their colleagues' feelings and perspectives, creating stronger and more supportive relationships.

2. Respect and Appreciation: Positive thinking encourages respect and appreciation for others. When employees feel respected and valued, they are more likely to reciprocate these feelings, leading to mutual respect and stronger relationships.

3. Effective Communication: Positive thinking improves communication by promoting active listening and constructive feedback. Employees who approach communication with a positive mindset are more likely to listen attentively, provide supportive feedback, and resolve conflicts amicably.

Strategies for Building Positive Work Relationships through Positive Thinking

1. PRACTICE ACTIVE Listening: Active listening involves fully focusing on the speaker, understanding their message, and responding thoughtfully. Encourage employees to practice active listening during interactions to foster understanding and empathy.

2. Show Appreciation and Gratitude: Regularly express appreciation and gratitude for colleagues' contributions and efforts. Positive reinforcement strengthens relationships and creates a supportive work environment.

3. Promote Open Communication: Encourage open and honest communication within the organization. Create opportunities for employees

to share their thoughts, ideas, and concerns. Positive thinking helps to create a safe space for open dialogue.

4. Resolve Conflicts Constructively: Approach conflicts with a solution-oriented mindset. Encourage employees to view conflicts as opportunities for growth and learning. Positive thinking fosters a collaborative approach to conflict resolution.

5. Foster Teamwork and Collaboration: Create opportunities for teamwork and collaboration. Encourage employees to work together on projects and initiatives. Positive thinking promotes a collaborative atmosphere where everyone feels valued and included.

6. Encourage Diversity and Inclusion: Promote a diverse and inclusive work environment where different perspectives are valued and respected. Positive thinking helps to appreciate and leverage this diversity for stronger work relationships.

7. Lead by Example: Leaders play a crucial role in building positive work relationships. Encourage leaders to model positive thinking, empathy, and respect in their interactions with employees.

Case Study: Building Positive Work Relationships at HealthCare Plus

HEALTHCARE PLUS, A healthcare organization, recognized the importance of positive work relationships for its overall success. The organization decided to implement a positive thinking approach to enhance relationships among its employees.

HealthCare Plus started by promoting active listening. Training sessions were conducted to teach employees the principles of active listening, and they were encouraged to practice these skills during interactions with colleagues and patients.

The organization also focused on showing appreciation and gratitude. Managers regularly expressed appreciation for employees' contributions and efforts through recognition programs and thank-you notes. This positive reinforcement strengthened relationships and boosted morale.

To promote open communication, HealthCare Plus created opportunities for employees to share their thoughts and ideas. Regular team meetings, suggestion boxes, and feedback sessions were introduced to facilitate open dialogue. Employees felt valued and heard, which enhanced their sense of belonging and motivation.

HealthCare Plus encouraged constructive conflict resolution. Training sessions on conflict management and resolution were provided, emphasizing a solution-oriented approach. Employees were encouraged to view conflicts as opportunities for growth and learning.

The organization fostered teamwork and collaboration by creating cross-functional teams for various projects and initiatives. Team-building activities and collaborative workspaces were introduced to encourage collaboration and strengthen relationships.

HealthCare Plus also promoted diversity and inclusion. The organization valued different perspectives and encouraged employees to appreciate and respect each other's uniqueness. Positive thinking helped to create an inclusive work environment where everyone felt valued.

Leaders at HealthCare Plus led by example, modeling positive thinking, empathy, and respect in their interactions with employees. Their leadership set the tone for a positive and supportive work culture.

As a result of these initiatives, HealthCare Plus saw a significant improvement in work relationships. Employees were more engaged, motivated, and collaborative. The positive thinking approach played a crucial role in creating a harmonious and supportive work environment.

Leadership and Positive Influence

EFFECTIVE LEADERSHIP is critical for organizational success, and positive thinking is a key attribute of successful leaders. Positive leaders inspire and motivate their teams, create a positive work environment, and drive organizational performance.

The Role of Positive Thinking in Leadership

POSITIVE THINKING ENHANCES leadership by fostering a vision of possibility, resilience, and empowerment. Positive leaders approach challenges with optimism, inspire their teams with a compelling vision, and create an environment where employees feel valued and motivated.

1. Inspiring Vision and Motivation: Positive leaders inspire their teams with a compelling vision of what is possible. They communicate this vision with enthusiasm and optimism, motivating employees to work towards common goals. Positive thinking helps leaders to maintain a hopeful outlook, even in challenging times, and inspire their teams to do the same.

2. Resilience and Adaptability: Positive thinking enhances resilience and adaptability in leaders. Positive leaders view challenges as opportunities for growth and learning, and they remain adaptable in the face of change. Their resilience sets an example for their teams and helps to create a culture of continuous improvement.

3. Empowerment and Support: Positive leaders empower their teams by providing support, resources, and opportunities for growth. They believe in their employees' potential and encourage them to take on new challenges and responsibilities. Positive thinking helps leaders to create an environment where employees feel empowered and motivated to excel.

Strategies for Positive Leadership and Influence

1. COMMUNICATE A POSITIVE Vision: Clearly communicate a positive and inspiring vision for the organization. Use positive language and enthusiasm to motivate employees and align them with the organization's goals.

2. Lead by Example: Model positive thinking, resilience, and adaptability in your leadership. Demonstrate optimism and a solution-oriented mindset in the face of challenges. Your behavior sets the tone for the entire organization.

3. Provide Support and Resources: Empower employees by providing the support and resources they need to succeed. Encourage their growth and development through training, mentoring, and opportunities for advancement.

4. Foster a Positive Work Environment: Create a positive and supportive work environment where employees feel valued and appreciated. Recognize and celebrate their achievements, provide constructive feedback, and encourage open communication.

5. Encourage Innovation and Risk-Taking: Foster a culture of innovation and risk-taking. Encourage employees to explore new ideas and approaches, and support them in their creative endeavors. Positive thinking helps to reduce fear of failure and promotes a growth mindset.

6. Build Strong Relationships: Build strong relationships with employees based on trust, empathy, and respect. Practice active listening, show appreciation, and address conflicts constructively. Positive relationships enhance teamwork and collaboration.

7. Promote Work-Life Balance: Support employees in achieving a healthy work-life balance. Promote flexible work arrangements, wellness programs, and time management skills. Positive thinking reinforces the importance of balance and self-care.

Case Study: Positive Leadership at GreenTech Innovations

GREENTECH INNOVATIONS, a renewable energy company, aimed to enhance its leadership approach to drive organizational success. The company decided to implement a positive thinking approach to leadership.

GreenTech Innovations started by communicating a positive vision. The CEO articulated a compelling vision of a sustainable future powered by renewable energy. This vision was communicated with enthusiasm and optimism, motivating employees to work towards common goals.

Leaders at GreenTech Innovations led by example, modeling positive thinking, resilience, and adaptability. They demonstrated optimism and a solution-oriented mindset in the face of challenges, setting an example for their teams.

The company provided support and resources to empower employees. Training programs, mentoring, and opportunities for advancement were introduced to encourage growth and development. Leaders believed in their employees' potential and supported them in taking on new challenges.

GreenTech Innovations focused on creating a positive work environment. Employee achievements were recognized and celebrated through regular appreciation events and feedback sessions. Open communication was encouraged, and employees felt valued and supported.

To foster innovation and risk-taking, GreenTech Innovations encouraged employees to explore new ideas and approaches. A culture of experimentation was promoted, where failures were seen as part of the learning process. Positive thinking helped to reduce fear of failure and promote a growth mindset.

Leaders at GreenTech Innovations built strong relationships with employees based on trust, empathy, and respect. Active listening, appreciation, and constructive conflict resolution were practiced to enhance teamwork and collaboration.

The company also promoted work-life balance by supporting flexible work arrangements and wellness programs. Employees were encouraged to manage their work responsibilities while maintaining their overall well-being.

As a result of these initiatives, GreenTech Innovations experienced significant improvements in organizational performance. Employees were more engaged, motivated, and innovative. The positive thinking approach to leadership played a crucial role in driving the company's success.

Conclusion

Positive thinking has a profound impact on the workplace, enhancing productivity and creativity, building positive work relationships, and fostering effective leadership. By cultivating a positive mindset, individuals and organizations can achieve greater success and create a thriving work environment.

Enhancing productivity through positive thinking involves fostering motivation, focus, and resilience. Strategies such as setting clear goals, creating a positive work environment, promoting work-life balance, and providing growth opportunities can boost productivity.

Building positive work relationships through positive thinking involves fostering empathy, respect, and effective communication. Strategies such as active listening, showing appreciation, promoting open communication, and encouraging teamwork can strengthen relationships.

Effective leadership through positive thinking involves inspiring vision, resilience, empowerment, and support. Strategies such as communicating a positive vision, leading by example, providing support and resources, fostering innovation, and building strong relationships can enhance leadership effectiveness.

By incorporating practical strategies for positive thinking, individuals and organizations can create a positive and supportive work environment, enhance performance, and achieve their goals. Remember, the journey to positive thinking in the workplace is unique for each individual and organization and requires ongoing effort and commitment. Embrace the process, be patient with yourself and your colleagues, and celebrate the positive changes that unfold. By nurturing a positive mindset, you can unlock the potential for a more meaningful and fulfilling work experience.

Chapter 12: The Power of Positive Thinking in Challenging Times

Navigating Life's Transitions

Life's transitions, whether expected or unexpected, can be daunting and disruptive. They often bring a mix of emotions, from excitement to anxiety, and require us to adapt to new circumstances. Positive thinking plays a crucial role in navigating these transitions by helping us approach change with optimism, resilience, and a proactive mindset.

Understanding Life's Transitions

LIFE'S TRANSITIONS can take many forms, including career changes, moving to a new location, starting or ending relationships, and significant life events such as marriage, parenthood, or retirement. Each transition presents unique challenges and opportunities, requiring us to adjust our routines, perspectives, and expectations.

Transitions can be categorized into two main types:

1. Planned Transitions: These are changes we anticipate and prepare for, such as graduating from college, starting a new job, or moving to a new home. Planned transitions often come with a sense of control and the opportunity to plan ahead.

2. Unplanned Transitions: These are unexpected changes that disrupt our lives, such as job loss, health crises, or the sudden death of a loved one. Unplanned transitions can be more challenging as they often involve uncertainty and a lack of control.

The Role of Positive Thinking in Navigating Transitions

POSITIVE THINKING IS a powerful tool for managing both planned and unplanned transitions. It helps us approach change with an open mind, maintain resilience in the face of challenges, and find opportunities for growth and learning.

1. Approaching Change with an Open Mind: Positive thinkers are more likely to embrace change and see it as an opportunity for growth rather than a threat. They approach transitions with curiosity and a willingness to explore new possibilities.

2. Maintaining Resilience: Resilience is the ability to bounce back from adversity. Positive thinking fosters resilience by helping individuals stay focused on solutions rather than problems. Resilient individuals are better equipped to handle the stress and uncertainty that often accompany transitions.

3. Finding Opportunities for Growth: Positive thinkers view transitions as opportunities for personal and professional growth. They are more likely to set new goals, seek out learning experiences, and adapt to new circumstances with confidence.

Strategies for Navigating Life's Transitions with Positive Thinking

1. EMBRACE CHANGE AS a Natural Part of Life: Accept that change is an inevitable part of life. Embracing this reality helps to reduce resistance and fosters a more positive attitude towards transitions.

2. Set Clear Goals and Priorities: Define clear goals and priorities for the transition period. Having a sense of direction and purpose helps to maintain focus and motivation.

3. Practice Self-Compassion: Be kind and compassionate towards yourself during times of transition. Acknowledge your feelings and give yourself permission to experience them without judgment.

4. Seek Support from Others: Reach out to friends, family members, or support groups for encouragement and guidance. Sharing your experiences and feelings with others can provide valuable perspectives and reduce feelings of isolation.

5. Focus on What You Can Control: Identify the aspects of the transition that you can influence and take proactive steps in those areas. Focusing on what you can control helps to reduce feelings of helplessness and empowers you to make meaningful progress.

6. Stay Open to New Opportunities: Approach the transition with an open mind and a willingness to explore new opportunities. Positive thinking helps to see the potential for growth and learning in every situation.

7. Maintain a Positive Routine: Establish a positive routine that includes self-care activities, such as exercise, meditation, and hobbies. A consistent routine provides stability and helps to manage stress.

Case Study: Sarah's Transition to a New City

SARAH, A YOUNG PROFESSIONAL, recently moved to a new city for a job opportunity. The transition was exciting but also filled with uncertainty and challenges. Sarah decided to adopt a positive thinking approach to navigate this major life change.

Sarah embraced the move as a natural part of her career growth. She set clear goals for her transition period, such as settling into her new apartment, making new friends, and excelling in her new job. These goals provided a sense of direction and purpose.

To manage her emotions, Sarah practiced self-compassion. She acknowledged her feelings of homesickness and anxiety without judgment and allowed herself time to adjust to the new environment.

Sarah sought support from her family and friends back home. She maintained regular contact with them through phone calls and video chats, which provided a sense of connection and encouragement.

Focusing on what she could control, Sarah took proactive steps to make her new city feel like home. She explored local attractions, joined social groups, and attended networking events to meet new people.

Staying open to new opportunities, Sarah viewed the transition as a chance for personal and professional growth. She enrolled in a local language course to learn the city's primary language and volunteered for community projects to build new skills.

Maintaining a positive routine, Sarah made time for self-care activities such as jogging in the park, practicing yoga, and pursuing her hobbies. This routine provided stability and helped her manage stress.

As a result of her positive thinking approach, Sarah successfully navigated her transition to the new city. She built a supportive network, excelled in her new job, and felt more confident and resilient in the face of change.

Building Resilience and Perseverance

RESILIENCE AND PERSEVERANCE are essential qualities for navigating life's challenges and achieving long-term success. Positive thinking plays a crucial role in building these qualities by fostering a mindset of strength, determination, and optimism.

Understanding Resilience and Perseverance

RESILIENCE IS THE ABILITY to recover from setbacks and adapt to adversity. It involves maintaining a positive outlook, staying focused on solutions, and bouncing back from difficult situations. Perseverance, on the other hand, is the determination to continue striving towards goals despite obstacles and setbacks. It involves sustained effort, commitment, and the ability to stay motivated over the long term.

The Role of Positive Thinking in Building Resilience

POSITIVE THINKING ENHANCES resilience by helping individuals stay focused on solutions, maintain hope, and learn from experiences. Resilient individuals are better equipped to handle stress, adapt to change, and overcome adversity.

1. Staying Focused on Solutions: Positive thinkers focus on finding solutions rather than dwelling on problems. This solution-oriented mindset helps to reduce stress and empowers individuals to take proactive steps in overcoming challenges.

2. Maintaining Hope and Optimism: Positive thinking fosters hope and optimism, which are essential for resilience. Hope provides the motivation to keep going, even in the face of adversity, while optimism helps to maintain a positive outlook on the future.

3. Learning from Experiences: Positive thinkers view setbacks and failures as opportunities for learning and growth. They reflect on their experiences, identify lessons learned, and use this knowledge to improve future outcomes.

The Role of Positive Thinking in Building Perseverance

POSITIVE THINKING ENHANCES perseverance by fostering a mindset of determination, self-belief, and sustained motivation. Perseverant individuals are more likely to stay committed to their goals and continue striving towards success.

1. Fostering Determination: Positive thinkers are determined to achieve their goals, even when faced with obstacles. They maintain a strong sense of purpose and are willing to put in the effort required to succeed.

2. Building Self-Belief: Positive thinking reinforces self-belief and confidence. Individuals who believe in their abilities are more likely to persevere through challenges and stay committed to their goals.

3. Sustaining Motivation: Positive thinking helps to sustain motivation over the long term. Positive affirmations, visualization, and goal-setting techniques can reinforce motivation and keep individuals focused on their aspirations.

Strategies for Building Resilience and Perseverance through Positive Thinking

1. PRACTICE POSITIVE Self-Talk: Use positive self-talk to reinforce self-belief and confidence. Replace negative thoughts with positive affirmations that support your goals and abilities.

2. Set Realistic and Achievable Goals: Set realistic and achievable goals that provide a sense of direction and purpose. Break down larger goals into smaller, manageable steps to maintain motivation and track progress.

3. Develop a Growth Mindset: Adopt a growth mindset by viewing challenges and setbacks as opportunities for learning and growth. Embrace the belief that you can improve and succeed through effort and perseverance.

4. Cultivate a Supportive Network: Surround yourself with supportive individuals who encourage and motivate you. Seek guidance and feedback from mentors, friends, and family members who believe in your potential.

5. Practice Mindfulness and Stress Management: Engage in mindfulness practices and stress management techniques to build resilience. Mindfulness meditation, deep breathing exercises, and physical activity can help to reduce stress and enhance emotional well-being.

6. Celebrate Small Victories: Celebrate small victories and achievements along the way. Acknowledging your progress reinforces motivation and builds confidence in your abilities.

7. Stay Flexible and Adaptable: Stay flexible and adaptable in the face of change. Be willing to adjust your plans and strategies as needed to overcome obstacles and continue moving forward.

Case Study: John's Journey to Overcome Adversity

JOHN, A SMALL BUSINESS owner, faced significant challenges when his business was impacted by an economic downturn. Sales declined, and he struggled to keep his business afloat. Determined to overcome adversity, John decided to adopt a positive thinking approach to build resilience and perseverance.

John practiced positive self-talk to reinforce his belief in his ability to turn his business around. He replaced negative thoughts with positive affirmations, such as "I have the skills and determination to overcome this challenge."

He set realistic and achievable goals for his business, such as reducing expenses, increasing marketing efforts, and improving customer service. John broke down these goals into smaller, manageable steps to maintain focus and track progress.

Adopting a growth mindset, John viewed the economic downturn as an opportunity for learning and improvement. He attended business workshops, sought advice from mentors, and implemented new strategies to adapt to the changing market conditions.

John cultivated a supportive network by seeking guidance and encouragement from fellow business owners, mentors, and his family. Their support provided valuable insights and motivation to persevere.

To manage stress and build resilience, John practiced mindfulness meditation and engaged in regular physical activity. These practices helped him stay calm and focused during challenging times.

John celebrated small victories, such as securing new customers and improving operational efficiency. Acknowledging these achievements reinforced his motivation and confidence.

Staying flexible and adaptable, John adjusted his business strategies as needed. He explored new revenue streams, diversified his product offerings, and embraced digital marketing to reach a broader audience.

As a result of his positive thinking approach, John successfully navigated the economic downturn and rebuilt his business. He emerged stronger and more resilient, with a renewed sense of determination and confidence.

Finding Hope in Difficult Situations

DIFFICULT SITUATIONS, whether personal, professional, or global, can be overwhelming and disheartening. Finding hope in these challenging times is essential for maintaining emotional well-being, resilience, and the motivation to keep moving forward. Positive thinking plays a crucial role in cultivating hope by fostering an optimistic outlook, reinforcing self-belief, and inspiring action.

Understanding Hope

HOPE IS THE BELIEF that positive outcomes are possible, even in the face of adversity. It provides the motivation to keep striving towards goals, the resilience to overcome challenges, and the strength to endure difficult times. Hope is a powerful force that can uplift and inspire individuals to persevere and achieve their aspirations.

The Role of Positive Thinking in Cultivating Hope

POSITIVE THINKING ENHANCES hope by promoting an optimistic outlook, reinforcing self-belief, and inspiring proactive behavior. Individuals who maintain a positive mindset are more likely to find hope and stay motivated, even in difficult situations.

1. Promoting an Optimistic Outlook: Positive thinkers maintain an optimistic outlook on the future. They believe that positive outcomes are possible and focus on potential solutions rather than problems. This optimism fosters hope and provides the motivation to keep moving forward.

2. Reinforcing Self-Belief: Positive thinking reinforces self-belief and confidence. Individuals who believe in their abilities are more likely to feel hopeful about their prospects and remain motivated to achieve their goals.

3. Inspiring Proactive Behavior: Positive thinking inspires proactive behavior and action. Hopeful individuals are more likely to take steps towards their goals, seek out opportunities, and make positive changes in their lives.

Strategies for Finding Hope through Positive Thinking

1. FOCUS ON POSITIVE Outcomes: Visualize and focus on positive outcomes rather than dwelling on negative possibilities. Use positive affirmations and visualization techniques to reinforce an optimistic outlook.

2. Set Meaningful Goals: Set meaningful and achievable goals that provide a sense of purpose and direction. Working towards these goals fosters hope and motivation.

3. Practice Gratitude: Cultivate a gratitude practice by regularly reflecting on and appreciating the positive aspects of your life. Gratitude fosters a positive mindset and reinforces hope.

4. Seek Inspirational Role Models: Look for inspirational role models who have overcome adversity and achieved success. Their stories can provide motivation and reinforce the belief that positive outcomes are possible.

5. Engage in Acts of Kindness: Engage in acts of kindness and support others in their challenges. Helping others fosters a sense of connection and reinforces hope for a better future.

6. Stay Connected to a Supportive Community: Surround yourself with supportive individuals who encourage and uplift you. A supportive community provides strength and reinforces hope.

7. Practice Mindfulness and Positive Reflection: Engage in mindfulness practices and positive reflection to stay grounded and focused on the present moment. Reflecting on past successes and positive experiences reinforces hope and confidence.

Case Study: Emma's Journey to Finding Hope

EMMA, A SINGLE MOTHER, faced significant challenges when she lost her job during a global economic crisis. Struggling to provide for her family, Emma felt overwhelmed and hopeless. Determined to find hope and overcome her difficulties, Emma decided to adopt a positive thinking approach.

Emma focused on positive outcomes by visualizing herself finding a new job and creating a stable future for her family. She used positive affirmations to reinforce her belief in her abilities and maintain an optimistic outlook.

She set meaningful and achievable goals, such as updating her resume, applying for jobs, and pursuing additional training to enhance her skills. Working towards these goals provided a sense of purpose and direction.

Emma practiced gratitude by reflecting on the positive aspects of her life, such as her supportive family and her health. This gratitude practice fostered a positive mindset and reinforced hope.

Seeking inspiration, Emma looked for role models who had overcome similar challenges. She read stories of individuals who had successfully rebuilt their lives after job loss, which provided motivation and reinforced the belief that positive outcomes were possible.

Emma engaged in acts of kindness by volunteering at a local food bank. Helping others in need provided a sense of connection and reinforced hope for a better future.

She stayed connected to a supportive community by reaching out to friends, family members, and support groups. Their encouragement and support provided strength and reinforced hope.

Practicing mindfulness and positive reflection, Emma stayed grounded and focused on the present moment. She reflected on her past successes and positive experiences, which reinforced her confidence and hope.

As a result of her positive thinking approach, Emma found a new job and created a stable future for her family. She emerged from the crisis with renewed hope, resilience, and determination.

Conclusion

Positive thinking is a powerful tool for navigating challenging times, building resilience and perseverance, and finding hope in difficult situations. By fostering an optimistic outlook, reinforcing self-belief, and inspiring proactive behavior, positive thinking empowers individuals to overcome adversity and achieve their goals.

Navigating life's transitions with positive thinking involves approaching change with an open mind, maintaining resilience, and finding opportunities for growth. Strategies such as embracing change, setting clear goals, practicing self-compassion, seeking support, focusing on what you can control, staying open to new opportunities, and maintaining a positive routine can help individuals navigate transitions successfully.

Building resilience and perseverance through positive thinking involves staying focused on solutions, maintaining hope and optimism, learning from experiences, fostering determination, building self-belief, and sustaining motivation. Strategies such as practicing positive self-talk, setting realistic goals, developing a growth mindset, cultivating a supportive network, practicing mindfulness, celebrating small victories, and staying flexible and adaptable can enhance resilience and perseverance.

Finding hope in difficult situations through positive thinking involves promoting an optimistic outlook, reinforcing self-belief, and inspiring proactive behavior. Strategies such as focusing on positive outcomes, setting meaningful goals, practicing gratitude, seeking inspirational role models, engaging in acts of kindness, staying connected to a supportive community, and practicing mindfulness and positive reflection can help individuals find hope and stay motivated.

By incorporating practical strategies for positive thinking, individuals can navigate challenging times with strength, resilience, and hope. Remember, the journey to positive thinking in challenging times is unique for each individual and requires ongoing effort and commitment. Embrace the process, be patient with yourself, and celebrate the positive changes that unfold. By nurturing a positive mindset, you can unlock the potential for a more meaningful and fulfilling life, even in the face of adversity.

Chapter 13: Teaching Positive Thinking to Others

Parenting with Positivity

Positive thinking is a powerful tool that can be imparted to others, and one of the most fundamental ways to do this is through parenting. Teaching children to approach life with optimism and resilience lays the foundation for their future success and well-being. Positive parenting fosters a supportive and nurturing environment where children can develop a strong sense of self-worth and confidence.

The Importance of Positive Parenting

POSITIVE PARENTING involves guiding and nurturing children with empathy, respect, and encouragement. It focuses on building a strong parent-child relationship based on trust and open communication. Positive parenting helps children develop emotional intelligence, self-esteem, and the ability to cope with challenges.

The Role of Positive Thinking in Parenting

POSITIVE THINKING IN parenting influences how parents interact with their children and respond to their needs. It involves adopting a hopeful and optimistic outlook, emphasizing strengths and possibilities, and fostering a growth mindset.

1. Modeling Positive Behavior: Children learn by observing their parents. Positive thinking parents model optimism and resilience in their behavior, showing children how to handle challenges with a positive attitude.

2. Encouraging a Growth Mindset: Positive thinking parents encourage a growth mindset, which is the belief that abilities and intelligence can be

developed through effort and learning. They praise effort and perseverance, helping children understand that setbacks are opportunities for growth.

3. Building Emotional Resilience: Positive thinking parents help children build emotional resilience by teaching them how to manage their emotions, cope with stress, and recover from setbacks. They provide a supportive environment where children feel safe to express their feelings and seek help when needed.

Strategies for Positive Parenting

1. COMMUNICATE POSITIVELY: Use positive language and affirmations when communicating with your children. Focus on their strengths and efforts rather than their shortcomings. Encourage open and honest communication, and listen actively to their concerns and feelings.

2. Set Realistic Expectations: Set realistic and achievable expectations for your children based on their abilities and developmental stage. Celebrate their achievements, no matter how small, and provide constructive feedback to help them improve.

3. Encourage Independence and Autonomy: Foster independence and autonomy by allowing children to make choices and take responsibility for their actions. Provide guidance and support, but also give them the freedom to learn from their experiences.

4. Create a Positive Home Environment: Create a home environment that is positive, supportive, and nurturing. Establish routines and traditions that promote family bonding and a sense of security. Encourage activities that promote creativity, curiosity, and learning.

5. Teach Problem-Solving Skills: Teach children problem-solving skills by guiding them through the process of identifying problems, brainstorming solutions, and evaluating outcomes. Encourage them to think critically and creatively when faced with challenges.

6.Practice Gratitude and Appreciation: Encourage children to practice gratitude and appreciation by regularly reflecting on the positive aspects of their lives. This practice fosters a positive mindset and helps them develop a sense of contentment and happiness.

Case Study: Lisa's Positive Parenting Approach

LISA, A MOTHER OF TWO young children, decided to adopt a positive thinking approach to parenting. She wanted to create a supportive and nurturing environment where her children could thrive and develop a strong sense of self-worth.

Lisa started by modeling positive behavior. She made a conscious effort to handle challenges with optimism and resilience, showing her children how to approach difficulties with a positive attitude. When faced with setbacks, she remained calm and focused on finding solutions.

She encouraged a growth mindset by praising her children's efforts and perseverance. When her daughter struggled with a difficult math problem, Lisa praised her for her hard work and encouraged her to keep trying. She emphasized that mistakes were opportunities for learning and growth.

Lisa helped her children build emotional resilience by teaching them how to manage their emotions. She provided a safe space for them to express their feelings and offered support and guidance when they felt overwhelmed. She also taught them relaxation techniques, such as deep breathing and mindfulness, to help them cope with stress.

Lisa communicated positively with her children, using affirmations and positive language. She focused on their strengths and efforts, providing constructive feedback when needed. She encouraged open and honest communication, actively listening to their concerns and feelings.

She set realistic expectations based on her children's abilities and developmental stage. Lisa celebrated their achievements, no matter how small, and provided guidance to help them improve. She also encouraged their independence and autonomy, allowing them to make choices and take responsibility for their actions.

Lisa created a positive home environment by establishing routines and traditions that promoted family bonding. They had regular family game nights, outdoor activities, and creative projects. She encouraged activities that promoted creativity, curiosity, and learning.

To teach problem-solving skills, Lisa guided her children through the process of identifying problems, brainstorming solutions, and evaluating outcomes. She encouraged them to think critically and creatively when faced with challenges.

Lisa also encouraged her children to practice gratitude and appreciation. They kept a gratitude journal where they wrote down things they were thankful for each day. This practice fostered a positive mindset and helped them develop a sense of contentment and happiness.

As a result of Lisa's positive parenting approach, her children developed a strong sense of self-worth, emotional resilience, and a positive outlook on life. They were more confident, independent, and capable of handling challenges with optimism and perseverance.

Mentoring and Coaching with Optimism

MENTORING AND COACHING are powerful tools for personal and professional development. Positive thinking plays a crucial role in these relationships by fostering a supportive and encouraging environment where individuals can grow and achieve their goals. Mentors and coaches who adopt an optimistic approach inspire confidence, motivation, and resilience in their mentees and clients.

The Importance of Mentoring and Coaching

MENTORING AND COACHING provide individuals with guidance, support, and feedback to help them achieve their personal and professional goals. These relationships can lead to increased self-awareness, improved skills, and greater success. Positive thinking enhances the effectiveness of mentoring and coaching by creating a positive and empowering atmosphere.

The Role of Positive Thinking in Mentoring and Coaching

POSITIVE THINKING IN mentoring and coaching involves adopting an optimistic and supportive mindset, emphasizing strengths and possibilities, and fostering a growth mindset. It helps mentors and coaches build strong, trusting relationships with their mentees and clients, and empowers them to achieve their goals.

1. Building Trust and Rapport: Positive thinking mentors and coaches build trust and rapport with their mentees and clients by showing genuine interest and empathy. They create a safe and supportive environment where individuals feel valued and understood.

2. Emphasizing Strengths and Possibilities: Positive thinking mentors and coaches focus on the strengths and potential of their mentees and clients. They provide constructive feedback that highlights areas for improvement while emphasizing the individual's capabilities and possibilities.

3. Fostering a Growth Mindset: Positive thinking mentors and coaches encourage a growth mindset by helping their mentees and clients view challenges as opportunities for learning and growth. They promote the belief that abilities and intelligence can be developed through effort and learning.

Strategies for Mentoring and Coaching with Optimism

1. ESTABLISH CLEAR Goals and Expectations: Work with your mentees and clients to establish clear goals and expectations for the mentoring or coaching relationship. Define specific, achievable objectives and create a plan to achieve them.

2. Use Positive Language and Affirmations: Use positive language and affirmations to reinforce your mentees' and clients' self-belief and confidence. Focus on their strengths and efforts, and provide constructive feedback that encourages growth and improvement.

3. Encourage Self-Reflection and Self-Awareness: Encourage your mentees and clients to engage in self-reflection and develop self-awareness. Help them

identify their strengths, weaknesses, and areas for growth. Positive thinking fosters a supportive environment for self-discovery and personal development.

4. Provide Support and Encouragement: Provide ongoing support and encouragement to your mentees and clients. Celebrate their achievements, no matter how small, and offer guidance and motivation when they face challenges. Positive thinking helps to maintain their motivation and resilience.

5. Promote a Solution-Oriented Mindset: Encourage your mentees and clients to adopt a solution-oriented mindset. Help them focus on finding solutions rather than dwelling on problems. Positive thinking fosters a proactive approach to overcoming challenges.

6. Foster Independence and Accountability: Foster independence and accountability by encouraging your mentees and clients to take ownership of their goals and actions. Provide guidance and support, but also give them the freedom to learn from their experiences.

7. Create a Positive and Empowering Environment: Create a positive and empowering environment where your mentees and clients feel safe to express their thoughts and feelings. Positive thinking helps to build trust and rapport, which are essential for effective mentoring and coaching.

Case Study: Alex's Mentoring Approach

ALEX, AN EXPERIENCED business professional, decided to become a mentor to help young entrepreneurs succeed. He adopted a positive thinking approach to mentoring, focusing on building trust, emphasizing strengths, and fostering a growth mindset.

Alex started by establishing clear goals and expectations with his mentees. He worked with them to define specific, achievable objectives and created a plan to achieve these goals. This provided a sense of direction and purpose for the mentoring relationship.

He used positive language and affirmations to reinforce his mentees' self-belief and confidence. Alex focused on their strengths and efforts, providing constructive feedback that encouraged growth and improvement. When a mentee faced a challenge, Alex emphasized their potential and capabilities, helping them stay motivated.

Alex encouraged self-reflection and self-awareness by guiding his mentees through regular reflection exercises. He helped them identify their strengths, weaknesses, and areas for growth. This self-discovery process fostered a supportive environment for personal and professional development.

Providing ongoing support and encouragement, Alex celebrated his mentees' achievements, no matter how small. He offered guidance and motivation when they faced challenges, helping them maintain their resilience and determination.

Alex promoted a solution-oriented mindset by encouraging his mentees to focus on finding solutions rather than dwelling on problems. He guided them through problem-solving processes and helped them develop critical and creative thinking skills.

To foster independence and accountability, Alex encouraged his mentees to take ownership of their goals and actions. He provided guidance and support but also gave them the freedom to learn from their experiences and make decisions independently.

Creating a positive and empowering environment, Alex built trust and rapport with his mentees. He showed genuine interest and empathy, creating a safe space where they felt valued and understood.

As a result of Alex's positive thinking approach to mentoring, his mentees experienced significant personal and professional growth. They developed greater self-awareness, confidence, and resilience. Alex's mentorship helped them achieve their goals and succeed in their entrepreneurial endeavors.

Community and Social Impact

POSITIVE THINKING EXTENDS beyond individual relationships and can have a profound impact on communities and society as a whole. Teaching positive thinking within communities fosters a culture of optimism, collaboration, and resilience, leading to positive social change and improved well-being for all members.

The Importance of Positive Thinking in Communities

COMMUNITIES THRIVE when their members adopt a positive mindset. Positive thinking fosters a sense of belonging, mutual support, and collective resilience. It encourages individuals to work together towards common goals, creating a positive and inclusive environment where everyone can flourish.

The Role of Positive Thinking in Community and Social Impact

POSITIVE THINKING IN communities involves promoting optimism, collaboration, and resilience among community members. It encourages individuals to contribute to the well-being of their community and work together to address common challenges.

1. Promoting Optimism and Hope: Positive thinking fosters a sense of optimism and hope within communities. It encourages members to believe in the possibility of positive change and to work towards creating a better future.

2. Encouraging Collaboration and Mutual Support: Positive thinking promotes collaboration and mutual support among community members. It encourages individuals to work together, share resources, and support one another in achieving common goals.

3. Building Collective Resilience: Positive thinking enhances collective resilience by helping communities cope with adversity and bounce back from challenges. It fosters a sense of solidarity and mutual aid, enabling communities to recover and thrive.

Strategies for Teaching Positive Thinking in Communities

1. ORGANIZE COMMUNITY Workshops and Events: Organize workshops and events that promote positive thinking and resilience. These

can include motivational talks, skill-building sessions, and community-building activities. Provide opportunities for members to learn and practice positive thinking techniques.

2. Create Supportive Networks and Groups: Establish supportive networks and groups within the community where members can share their experiences, challenges, and successes. Encourage open communication and mutual support. Positive thinking fosters a sense of belonging and solidarity.

3. Promote Volunteerism and Community Service: Encourage community members to engage in volunteerism and community service. Volunteering provides a sense of purpose and fulfillment, fostering a positive mindset and contributing to the well-being of the community.

4. Celebrate Community Achievements: Recognize and celebrate the achievements and contributions of community members. Highlight success stories and positive examples that inspire and motivate others. Positive reinforcement builds a sense of pride and optimism.

5. Foster Inclusive and Diverse Environments: Promote inclusivity and diversity within the community. Encourage members to appreciate and respect different perspectives and backgrounds. Positive thinking helps to create an inclusive environment where everyone feels valued.

6. Provide Resources and Support for Mental Health: Provide resources and support for mental health and well-being. Offer access to counseling, support groups, and educational materials on positive thinking and resilience. Positive mental health fosters a stronger and more resilient community.

7. Encourage Positive Communication: Encourage positive communication and conflict resolution within the community. Promote active listening, empathy, and constructive feedback. Positive communication enhances relationships and builds a supportive environment.

Case Study: The Community of Hope Initiative

THE COMMUNITY OF HOPE Initiative was launched in a small town to promote positive thinking and resilience among its residents. The initiative aimed to create a supportive and inclusive environment where community members could thrive and work together towards common goals.

The initiative started by organizing community workshops and events focused on positive thinking and resilience. Motivational speakers, skill-building sessions, and community-building activities were offered to provide opportunities for learning and practice. Residents learned techniques for positive self-talk, goal setting, and stress management.

Supportive networks and groups were established within the community. Residents formed support groups where they could share their experiences, challenges, and successes. These groups fostered open communication and mutual support, creating a sense of belonging and solidarity.

The Community of Hope Initiative promoted volunteerism and community service. Residents were encouraged to engage in volunteer activities that aligned with their interests and skills. Volunteering provided a sense of purpose and fulfillment, fostering a positive mindset and contributing to the well-being of the community.

Community achievements were recognized and celebrated through regular events and publications. Success stories and positive examples were highlighted to inspire and motivate others. Positive reinforcement built a sense of pride and optimism among residents.

Inclusivity and diversity were promoted within the community. The initiative encouraged residents to appreciate and respect different perspectives and backgrounds. Positive thinking helped to create an inclusive environment where everyone felt valued.

Resources and support for mental health and well-being were provided. The initiative offered access to counseling, support groups, and educational materials on positive thinking and resilience. These resources fostered a stronger and more resilient community.

Positive communication and conflict resolution were encouraged within the community. Residents were taught active listening, empathy, and constructive feedback techniques. Positive communication enhanced relationships and built a supportive environment.

As a result of the Community of Hope Initiative, the town experienced significant improvements in overall well-being and social cohesion. Residents developed greater resilience, optimism, and a sense of community. The positive thinking approach created a supportive and inclusive environment where everyone could thrive.

Conclusion

Teaching positive thinking to others is a powerful way to foster individual and collective well-being. By incorporating positive thinking into parenting, mentoring and coaching, and community initiatives, we can create supportive and empowering environments where individuals can thrive and achieve their goals.

Positive parenting involves modeling positive behavior, encouraging a growth mindset, and building emotional resilience. Strategies such as positive communication, setting realistic expectations, fostering independence, creating a positive home environment, teaching problem-solving skills, and practicing gratitude can help parents teach positive thinking to their children.

Mentoring and coaching with optimism involve building trust and rapport, emphasizing strengths and possibilities, and fostering a growth mindset. Strategies such as establishing clear goals, using positive language and affirmations, encouraging self-reflection, providing support and encouragement, promoting a solution-oriented mindset, fostering independence, and creating a positive environment can enhance the effectiveness of mentoring and coaching.

Teaching positive thinking in communities involves promoting optimism, collaboration, and resilience. Strategies such as organizing workshops and events, creating supportive networks, promoting volunteerism, celebrating achievements, fostering inclusivity, providing mental health resources, and encouraging positive communication can lead to positive social change and improved well-being for all community members.

By incorporating practical strategies for teaching positive thinking, we can create a ripple effect that enhances individual and collective well-being. Remember, the journey to teaching positive thinking is unique for each individual and community and requires ongoing effort and commitment. Embrace the process, be patient with yourself and others, and celebrate the positive changes that unfold. By nurturing a positive mindset, you can unlock the potential for a more meaningful and fulfilling life for yourself and those around you.

Chapter 14: Stories of Transformation Through Positive Thinking

Inspirational Case Studies

Positive thinking has the power to transform lives. This chapter explores inspirational case studies that illustrate how adopting a positive mindset can lead to profound personal and professional transformations. These stories demonstrate the resilience, determination, and optimism of individuals who have harnessed the power of positive thinking to overcome adversity and achieve success.

Case Study 1: Overcoming Personal Adversity

BACKGROUND

Rachel, a 34-year-old marketing professional, faced a series of personal adversities that seemed insurmountable. Following a difficult divorce and the sudden loss of her mother, Rachel found herself struggling with grief, depression, and a sense of hopelessness. She had always been a high achiever, but these events left her feeling lost and unable to move forward.

Transformation Through Positive Thinking

RACHEL'S JOURNEY OF transformation began when she decided to seek help through therapy. Her therapist introduced her to the principles of positive thinking and encouraged her to incorporate them into her daily life.

1. Adopting a Positive Mindset: Rachel started by changing her internal dialogue. Instead of focusing on her losses, she began to remind herself of her strengths and the possibilities for her future. She kept a journal where she wrote down positive affirmations and reflected on her achievements, no matter how small.

2. Setting Realistic Goals: Rachel set small, achievable goals for herself, starting with basic self-care activities like getting out of bed, exercising, and eating healthily. As she met these goals, she set more ambitious ones, such as reconnecting with friends and pursuing professional development opportunities.

3. Finding New Purpose: To find a new sense of purpose, Rachel volunteered at a local shelter. Helping others provided her with a sense of fulfillment and shifted her focus away from her own pain. She also started taking online courses in digital marketing to enhance her skills and stay current in her field.

4. Building a Support Network: Rachel reconnected with friends and family, sharing her journey and allowing them to support her. She also joined support groups for people dealing with grief and loss, where she found understanding and encouragement.

Outcome

Rachel's positive thinking approach led to significant changes in her life. She gradually overcame her depression and regained her confidence. Her efforts in professional development paid off, and she was promoted at work. More importantly, Rachel found a new sense of purpose and joy in her life. Her story is a testament to the transformative power of positive thinking in overcoming personal adversity.

Case Study 2: Professional Rebirth

BACKGROUND

James, a 45-year-old software engineer, faced a professional crisis when he was laid off from his job of 15 years due to company downsizing. This unexpected change left him feeling insecure and doubtful about his future. With a family to support and a mortgage to pay, James needed to find a way to turn his situation around quickly.

Transformation Through Positive Thinking

JAMES DECIDED TO APPROACH his situation with a positive mindset, focusing on the opportunities that lay ahead rather than the setback he had experienced.

1. Embracing Change: Instead of viewing his layoff as a failure, James saw it as an opportunity to reinvent himself. He took time to reflect on his career and identify his passions and strengths. He realized that he had always been interested in cybersecurity, a field with growing demand.

2. Upskilling and Education: James enrolled in online courses to gain certifications in cybersecurity. He viewed each course as a step towards his new career, maintaining a positive attitude even when the coursework was challenging.

3. Networking and Mentorship: James reached out to former colleagues and industry professionals, seeking advice and mentorship. He joined professional organizations and attended networking events, where he met individuals who provided guidance and support.

4. Positive Self-Talk and Visualization: Throughout his journey, James practiced positive self-talk, reminding himself of his abilities and potential. He also used visualization techniques, imagining himself succeeding in his new career.

Outcome

James successfully transitioned into a new career in cybersecurity. His positive mindset and proactive approach led to several job offers, and he eventually accepted a position at a leading tech company. James's story highlights the power of positive thinking in turning professional setbacks into opportunities for growth and success.

Case Study 3: Health and Wellness Transformation

BACKGROUND

Laura, a 52-year-old mother of three, had struggled with obesity and related health issues for most of her adult life. She had tried numerous diets and exercise programs, but her efforts always seemed to end in frustration and failure. Her weight was affecting her self-esteem, health, and overall quality of life.

Transformation Through Positive Thinking

LAURA'S TRANSFORMATION began when she decided to adopt a holistic approach to health and wellness, focusing on positive thinking and sustainable lifestyle changes.

1. Changing Her Mindset: Laura realized that her negative self-talk was sabotaging her efforts. She started practicing positive affirmations and focusing on what her body could do rather than its limitations. She celebrated small victories, such as completing a walk around the block or choosing a healthy meal.

2. Setting Realistic and Sustainable Goals: Instead of aiming for rapid weight loss, Laura set realistic and sustainable goals. She focused on making small, incremental changes to her diet and exercise routine. This approach made her goals more achievable and less overwhelming.

3. Finding Enjoyable Activities: Laura discovered that she enjoyed swimming and dancing. She incorporated these activities into her routine, which made exercise feel less like a chore and more like a fun and rewarding experience.

4. Building a Support System: Laura joined a local wellness group where she met others with similar goals. The group provided encouragement, accountability, and a sense of community. She also enlisted the support of her family, who joined her in making healthier choices.

Outcome

Over time, Laura achieved significant weight loss and improved her overall health. She felt more energetic, confident, and happy. Laura's story demonstrates how positive thinking and a holistic approach to health can lead to lasting transformation and improved well-being.

Personal Anecdotes of Success

PERSONAL ANECDOTES offer a glimpse into the everyday applications of positive thinking and how it can lead to success in various aspects of life. These stories, drawn from individuals' experiences, highlight the practical ways in which a positive mindset can overcome challenges and achieve goals.

Anecdote 1: Overcoming Academic Challenges

BACKGROUND

Sam, a high school student, struggled with math throughout his academic career. His low grades and frequent frustration led him to believe that he was simply not good at math. This negative mindset affected his confidence and performance in other subjects as well.

Turning Point

SAM'S TURNING POINT came when his math teacher introduced him to positive thinking techniques. She encouraged him to change his internal dialogue and approach math with a growth mindset.

Transformation

1. Positive Affirmations: Sam began each study session by repeating positive affirmations such as "I am capable of learning math" and "I can solve problems with practice." These affirmations helped shift his mindset from one of defeat to one of possibility.

2. Setting Incremental Goals: Sam set small, achievable goals for each study session, such as mastering a specific type of math problem. Each accomplishment boosted his confidence and motivated him to tackle more challenging topics.

3. Seeking Help and Collaboration: Sam started attending after-school tutoring sessions and formed study groups with classmates. Collaborating with peers and seeking help when needed reinforced the idea that it was okay to struggle and that he could improve with effort.

4. Visualizing Success: Before exams, Sam practiced visualization techniques, imagining himself confidently solving problems and earning good grades. This mental rehearsal helped reduce his anxiety and improve his performance.

Outcome

By the end of the school year, Sam's math grades improved significantly. More importantly, he developed a newfound confidence in his ability to learn and succeed in challenging subjects. His experience with positive thinking in math carried over to other areas of his life, leading to overall academic and personal growth.

Anecdote 2: Career Advancement Through Optimism

BACKGROUND

Emma, a mid-level manager at a marketing firm, felt stuck in her career. Despite her hard work and dedication, she had not received a promotion in several years. She began to doubt her abilities and considered looking for opportunities elsewhere.

Turning Point

EMMA'S TURNING POINT came when she attended a professional development workshop focused on positive thinking and leadership. Inspired by the workshop, she decided to adopt a more optimistic approach to her career.

Transformation

1. Positive Self-Talk: Emma replaced her self-doubt with positive self-talk, reminding herself of her strengths and accomplishments. She frequently

repeated affirmations such as "I am a valuable asset to my team" and "I am capable of leading and inspiring others."

2. Proactive Goal Setting: Emma set specific career goals, such as improving her leadership skills and taking on more challenging projects. She created a plan to achieve these goals, including attending additional training sessions and seeking feedback from her supervisors.

3. Building Relationships: Emma focused on building positive relationships with her colleagues and supervisors. She offered support and encouragement to her team, which fostered a more collaborative and productive work environment.

4. Visualizing Success: Emma visualized herself in a leadership role, confidently managing projects and guiding her team to success. This mental imagery helped boost her confidence and motivated her to take on new responsibilities.

Outcome

Within a year, Emma was promoted to a senior management position. Her positive thinking approach not only advanced her career but also improved her overall job satisfaction and work-life balance. Emma's story illustrates how optimism and proactive goal-setting can lead to career advancement and professional fulfillment.

Anecdote 3: Personal Growth Through Positive Thinking

BACKGROUND

Jake, a 28-year-old artist, struggled with self-doubt and fear of failure. Despite his talent and passion for art, he hesitated to showcase his work publicly. His fear of rejection held him back from pursuing his dream of becoming a professional artist.

Turning Point

JAKE'S TURNING POINT came when he attended an art retreat that emphasized the importance of positive thinking and self-belief. Inspired by the retreat, he decided to adopt a more positive mindset and take steps towards his dream.

Transformation

1. Embracing a Growth Mindset: Jake adopted a growth mindset, viewing each artistic challenge as an opportunity to learn and improve. He reminded himself that every great artist had faced rejection and setbacks on their journey to success.

2. Positive Affirmations: Jake used positive affirmations to combat his self-doubt. He repeated statements like "I am a talented artist" and "My work has value and meaning." These affirmations helped boost his confidence and reduce his fear of failure.

3. Taking Risks: Jake decided to take risks by submitting his work to local galleries and online platforms. He viewed each submission as a step towards his goal, regardless of the outcome. This proactive approach helped him overcome his fear of rejection.

4. Visualizing Success: Jake visualized himself as a successful artist, with his work displayed in galleries and appreciated by audiences. This mental imagery provided motivation and reinforced his belief in his potential.

Outcome

Jake's positive thinking approach led to significant personal growth. He successfully showcased his work in several local galleries and received positive feedback from art enthusiasts and critics. Jake's story demonstrates how embracing a growth mindset and taking risks can lead to personal and professional success.

Lessons Learned from Positive Thinkers

THE STORIES OF TRANSFORMATION through positive thinking offer valuable lessons that can be applied to various aspects of life. These lessons highlight the importance of mindset, resilience, and proactive behavior in achieving success and overcoming challenges.

Lesson 1: Mindset Matters

A POSITIVE MINDSET is a powerful tool for personal and professional growth. It shapes how we perceive and respond to challenges, influencing our behavior and outcomes. Adopting a positive mindset involves:

- Replacing negative self-talk with positive affirmations.

- Viewing challenges as opportunities for growth and learning.

- Focusing on strengths and possibilities rather than limitations.

Lesson 2: Resilience is Key

RESILIENCE IS THE ABILITY to bounce back from setbacks and adapt to change. Positive thinkers demonstrate resilience by maintaining hope and optimism, even in difficult situations. Building resilience involves:

- Practicing self-compassion and acknowledging your feelings.

- Setting realistic and achievable goals.

- Seeking support from others and building a strong support network.

- Staying focused on solutions and taking proactive steps to overcome challenges.

Lesson 3: Proactive Behavior Leads to Success

TAKING PROACTIVE STEPS towards your goals is essential for achieving success. Positive thinkers take initiative, set clear goals, and create actionable plans. Being proactive involves:

- Setting specific, achievable goals and creating a plan to achieve them.

- Seeking opportunities for learning and growth.

- Taking risks and embracing new challenges.

- Visualizing success and staying motivated.

Lesson 4: Support Networks are Crucial

HAVING A STRONG SUPPORT network is vital for personal and professional growth. Positive thinkers build and maintain supportive relationships that provide encouragement and guidance. Building a support network involves:

- Reaching out to friends, family, and colleagues for support and advice.

- Joining groups and communities with similar goals and interests.

- Offering support and encouragement to others.

- Celebrating achievements and milestones together.

Lesson 5: Gratitude and Positivity Foster Well-Being

PRACTICING GRATITUDE and maintaining a positive outlook contribute to overall well-being and happiness. Positive thinkers cultivate gratitude by focusing on the positive aspects of their lives. Practicing gratitude involves:

- Keeping a gratitude journal and regularly reflecting on things you are thankful for.

- Expressing appreciation and gratitude to others.

- Celebrating small victories and positive experiences.

- Focusing on the present moment and finding joy in everyday activities.

Lesson 6: Continuous Learning and Growth

CONTINUOUS LEARNING and growth are essential for achieving long-term success. Positive thinkers embrace a growth mindset and seek opportunities for self-improvement. Continuous learning involves:

- Setting goals for personal and professional development.

- Seeking feedback and using it to improve.

- Embracing new experiences and challenges.

- Staying curious and open to learning.

Lesson 7: Positive Thinking is a Practice

POSITIVE THINKING IS not a one-time effort but an ongoing practice that requires dedication and consistency. Maintaining a positive mindset involves:

- Regularly practicing positive self-talk and affirmations.

- Engaging in activities that promote well-being and happiness.

- Reflecting on your progress and adjusting your approach as needed.

- Staying committed to your goals and maintaining a positive outlook.

Conclusion

The stories of transformation through positive thinking illustrate the profound impact that a positive mindset can have on various aspects of life. These inspirational case studies and personal anecdotes highlight the resilience, determination, and optimism of individuals who have harnessed the power of positive thinking to overcome adversity and achieve success.

From overcoming personal adversity and professional setbacks to achieving health and wellness goals, these stories demonstrate that positive thinking is a powerful tool for personal and professional growth. The lessons learned from positive thinkers provide valuable insights into the importance of mindset, resilience, proactive behavior, support networks, gratitude, continuous learning, and the practice of positive thinking.

By incorporating these lessons into our own lives, we can unlock the potential for transformation and achieve greater success and fulfillment. Remember, the journey to positive thinking is unique for each individual and requires ongoing effort and commitment. Embrace the process, be patient with yourself, and celebrate the positive changes that unfold. By nurturing a positive mindset, you can unlock the potential for a more meaningful and fulfilling life.

Chapter 15: Maintaining a Positive Outlook for Life

Sustaining Positive Habits

Maintaining a positive outlook for life requires more than an initial commitment to change; it involves the sustained practice of positive habits that reinforce optimism and resilience over time. Developing and nurturing these habits is essential for embedding positive thinking into your daily routine and overall lifestyle.

The Importance of Sustaining Positive Habits

SUSTAINING POSITIVE habits helps to solidify the benefits of a positive mindset and ensures that it becomes an integral part of your life. Consistent practice of these habits fosters emotional well-being, enhances mental health, and contributes to long-term success and happiness.

Key Positive Habits to Cultivate

1. GRATITUDE PRACTICE: Regularly expressing gratitude helps to shift your focus from what you lack to what you have. Keeping a gratitude journal, where you write down three things you are grateful for each day, can significantly enhance your overall outlook on life.

2. Mindfulness and Meditation: Practicing mindfulness and meditation helps you stay grounded in the present moment. It reduces stress, improves focus, and fosters a sense of inner peace. Even a few minutes of daily meditation can have profound effects on your mental well-being.

3. Positive Affirmations: Using positive affirmations reinforces a positive self-image and boosts confidence. Start your day with affirmations that reflect

your goals and values, such as "I am capable and resilient" or "I embrace new opportunities with confidence."

4. Physical Activity: Regular physical activity is not only good for your body but also for your mind. Exercise releases endorphins, which are natural mood lifters. Find activities that you enjoy, whether it's walking, yoga, dancing, or swimming, and incorporate them into your routine.

5. Healthy Eating: A balanced diet rich in nutrients supports both physical and mental health. Eating a variety of fruits, vegetables, whole grains, and lean proteins helps to maintain energy levels and overall well-being.

6. Sleep Hygiene: Prioritizing good sleep hygiene is crucial for maintaining a positive outlook. Ensure that you get enough restful sleep by establishing a regular sleep schedule, creating a relaxing bedtime routine, and minimizing distractions in your sleep environment.

7. Social Connections: Maintaining strong social connections is essential for emotional support and overall happiness. Spend time with family and friends, engage in meaningful conversations, and participate in social activities that bring joy and fulfillment.

8. Continuous Learning: Lifelong learning keeps your mind engaged and fosters a sense of purpose. Pursue new skills, hobbies, and interests that excite you and contribute to your personal and professional growth.

Strategies for Sustaining Positive Habits

1. SET CLEAR INTENTIONS: Define clear intentions for the positive habits you want to cultivate. Understand why these habits are important to you and how they will contribute to your overall well-being.

2. Start Small and Build Gradually: Begin with small, manageable steps to avoid feeling overwhelmed. Gradually increase the complexity and frequency of your positive habits as they become more ingrained in your routine.

3. Create a Routine: Establish a daily routine that incorporates your positive habits. Consistency is key to making these habits a natural part of your life. For

example, you could practice gratitude journaling every morning or meditate for a few minutes before bed.

4. Track Your Progress: Keep track of your progress by maintaining a journal or using a habit-tracking app. Celebrate your achievements and milestones, no matter how small, to stay motivated and encouraged.

5. Seek Accountability: Share your goals and intentions with a trusted friend, family member, or mentor. Having someone to hold you accountable and provide support can help you stay committed to your positive habits.

6. Adjust as Needed: Be flexible and willing to adjust your habits as needed. Life is dynamic, and your needs and circumstances may change over time. Adapt your habits to fit your current situation and maintain a positive outlook.

Case Study: Maria's Journey to Sustaining Positive Habits

MARIA, A 38-YEAR-OLD teacher, decided to adopt positive habits to enhance her overall well-being and maintain a positive outlook on life. She started by identifying the habits that were most important to her and setting clear intentions for each.

Maria began with a gratitude practice, writing down three things she was grateful for each morning. This simple habit helped her start the day with a positive mindset and appreciate the good in her life.

She also incorporated mindfulness and meditation into her routine, dedicating ten minutes each evening to quiet reflection. This practice helped her manage stress and stay grounded in the present moment.

Maria found joy in physical activity by joining a local dance class. Dancing not only kept her physically active but also brought her happiness and a sense of community.

To support her physical and mental health, Maria focused on healthy eating and sleep hygiene. She prepared balanced meals with plenty of fruits and vegetables and established a regular sleep schedule that allowed her to get enough restful sleep.

Maria maintained strong social connections by spending quality time with her family and friends. She organized regular gatherings and participated in social activities that strengthened her relationships and provided emotional support.

Continuous learning was also important to Maria. She pursued her passion for painting by taking art classes and exploring new techniques. This hobby kept her mind engaged and provided a creative outlet.

Maria tracked her progress by keeping a journal, where she documented her daily habits and reflected on her experiences. She celebrated her achievements and made adjustments to her routine as needed.

With the support of her accountability partner, a close friend who shared similar goals, Maria stayed committed to her positive habits. Together, they encouraged each other and shared their successes and challenges.

As a result of her sustained positive habits, Maria experienced significant improvements in her overall well-being. She felt more energetic, confident, and content. Her journey demonstrates the power of maintaining positive habits to foster a positive outlook on life.

Reflecting on Your Journey

REFLECTION IS A POWERFUL tool for personal growth and self-awareness. Taking time to reflect on your journey allows you to evaluate your progress, celebrate your achievements, and learn from your experiences. Reflection helps you stay connected to your goals and values, reinforcing your commitment to maintaining a positive outlook on life.

The Importance of Reflection

REFLECTING ON YOUR journey provides valuable insights into your strengths, challenges, and areas for growth. It helps you understand the impact of your actions and decisions, guiding you towards continuous improvement. Reflection also fosters gratitude and appreciation for your accomplishments, reinforcing a positive mindset.

Ways to Reflect on Your Journey

1. JOURNALING: KEEPING a journal is an effective way to document your thoughts, feelings, and experiences. Writing about your journey helps you process your emotions, track your progress, and gain clarity on your goals and aspirations.

2. Meditation and Mindfulness: Engaging in meditation and mindfulness practices allows you to reflect on your journey with a calm and focused mind. These practices help you stay present and gain deeper insights into your experiences.

3. Self-Assessment: Conduct regular self-assessments to evaluate your progress towards your goals. Reflect on what has worked well, what challenges you have faced, and what changes you can make to improve.

4. Vision Boards: Creating a vision board is a visual way to reflect on your journey and stay connected to your goals. Include images, quotes, and symbols that represent your aspirations and achievements.

5. Discussion with a Mentor or Coach: Having discussions with a mentor or coach provides an external perspective on your journey. They can offer guidance, support, and constructive feedback to help you stay on track.

6. Gratitude Practice: Incorporating gratitude into your reflection helps you focus on the positive aspects of your journey. Reflect on what you are grateful for and how these experiences have contributed to your growth.

Questions to Guide Your Reflection

1. WHAT ARE MY KEY achievements and milestones?: Reflect on the significant accomplishments and milestones you have reached. Celebrate these successes and acknowledge the effort and dedication that made them possible.

2. What challenges have I faced and how have I overcome them?: Consider the obstacles and challenges you have encountered. Reflect on the strategies and resources you used to overcome them and what you learned from these experiences.

3. What have I learned about myself?: Reflect on the insights you have gained about your strengths, values, and areas for growth. Consider how these insights have influenced your actions and decisions.

4. How have my goals and priorities evolved?: Reflect on how your goals and priorities have changed over time. Consider the factors that have influenced these changes and how they align with your overall vision for your life.

5. What positive habits have I developed?: Reflect on the positive habits you have cultivated and how they have contributed to your well-being. Consider how you can continue to sustain and strengthen these habits.

6. What am I grateful for?: Reflect on the people, experiences, and opportunities that you are grateful for. Consider how these elements have enriched your life and contributed to your positive outlook.

Case Study: Reflecting on John's Journey

JOHN, A 45-YEAR-OLD entrepreneur, decided to take time to reflect on his journey of personal and professional growth. He used various reflection techniques to gain insights into his experiences and stay connected to his goals.

John kept a journal where he documented his thoughts, feelings, and experiences. Writing in his journal helped him process his emotions and gain clarity on his goals and aspirations. He regularly reviewed his journal entries to track his progress and identify patterns in his behavior.

Engaging in meditation and mindfulness practices allowed John to reflect on his journey with a calm and focused mind. He dedicated time each morning to meditate and practice mindfulness, which helped him stay present and gain deeper insights into his experiences.

John conducted regular self-assessments to evaluate his progress towards his goals. He reflected on what had worked well, what challenges he had faced, and what changes he could make to improve. These self-assessments guided his decision-making and actions.

Creating a vision board was a visual way for John to reflect on his journey and stay connected to his goals. He included images, quotes, and symbols that represented his aspirations and achievements. The vision board served as a daily reminder of his goals and progress.

Having discussions with his mentor provided John with an external perspective on his journey. His mentor offered guidance, support, and constructive feedback, helping John stay on track and make informed decisions.

Incorporating gratitude into his reflection helped John focus on the positive aspects of his journey. He reflected on what he was grateful for and how these experiences had contributed to his growth. This gratitude practice reinforced his positive mindset and appreciation for his accomplishments.

By reflecting on his journey, John gained valuable insights into his strengths, challenges, and areas for growth. He celebrated his achievements, learned from his experiences, and stayed connected to his goals and values. John's reflection practices helped him maintain a positive outlook on life and continue his journey of personal and professional growth.

Looking Forward: Continuing Your Transformation

MAINTAINING A POSITIVE outlook for life is an ongoing journey that requires continuous effort and commitment. Looking forward, it is essential to build on your positive habits, set new goals, and stay open to opportunities for growth and transformation.

Setting New Goals

SETTING NEW GOALS HELPS to keep you motivated and focused on your personal and professional growth. These goals should be specific, measurable, achievable, relevant, and time-bound (SMART).

1. Identify Your Aspirations: Reflect on your long-term vision for your life and identify the aspirations that are most important to you. Consider areas such as career, relationships, health, personal development, and contribution to society.

2. Break Down Your Goals: Break down your long-term aspirations into smaller, manageable goals. Create a roadmap that outlines the steps needed to achieve each goal. This approach makes your goals more achievable and provides a clear path forward.

3. Stay Flexible and Adaptable: Life is dynamic, and your goals may need to evolve over time. Stay flexible and adaptable, and be willing to adjust your goals as needed. Continuously reassess your priorities and make changes that align with your overall vision.

4. Celebrate Milestones: Celebrate the milestones and achievements along the way. Recognizing your progress reinforces your motivation and commitment to your goals.

Staying Open to Opportunities

OPENNESS TO NEW OPPORTUNITIES is essential for continuous growth and transformation. Embrace a mindset of curiosity and exploration, and be willing to take risks and try new things.

1. Seek New Experiences: Actively seek out new experiences that challenge you and broaden your horizons. This could include traveling, learning new skills, pursuing hobbies, or taking on new responsibilities at work.

2. Embrace Change: View change as an opportunity for growth rather than a threat. Embrace new opportunities with an open mind and a positive attitude. Be willing to step outside your comfort zone and explore new possibilities.

3. Network and Connect: Build and maintain a network of supportive individuals who inspire and motivate you. Engage in meaningful conversations, attend events, and join groups that align with your interests and goals.

4. Learn Continuously: Commit to lifelong learning and personal development. Pursue opportunities for education, training, and self-improvement. Stay curious and open to new knowledge and perspectives.

Cultivating Resilience

RESILIENCE IS THE ABILITY to adapt to challenges and bounce back from setbacks. Cultivating resilience is essential for maintaining a positive outlook on life and continuing your transformation.

1. Build a Support System: Surround yourself with supportive friends, family, and mentors who provide encouragement and guidance. A strong support system helps you navigate challenges and stay resilient.

2. Practice Self-Care: Prioritize self-care to maintain your physical, mental, and emotional well-being. Engage in activities that nourish your body and mind, such as exercise, meditation, hobbies, and relaxation.

3. Develop Coping Strategies: Develop healthy coping strategies to manage stress and adversity. This could include mindfulness practices, deep breathing exercises, journaling, and seeking professional support when needed.

4. Maintain a Positive Mindset: Continue to practice positive thinking and reinforce your positive habits. Focus on your strengths, celebrate your achievements, and stay optimistic about the future.

Case Study: Sophia's Continued Transformation

SOPHIA, A 30-YEAR-OLD nurse, had successfully adopted positive habits and maintained a positive outlook on life. Looking forward, she decided to continue her transformation by setting new goals, staying open to opportunities, and cultivating resilience.

Sophia identified her long-term aspirations, which included advancing her career, improving her health, and contributing to her community. She broke down these aspirations into smaller, manageable goals, creating a roadmap that outlined the steps needed to achieve each goal.

To advance her career, Sophia set a goal to pursue a specialized nursing certification. She researched available programs, enrolled in a course, and dedicated time each week to study. She also sought mentorship from experienced colleagues who provided guidance and support.

Sophia stayed open to new opportunities by seeking new experiences that challenged her and broadened her horizons. She volunteered for medical missions abroad, which allowed her to gain new skills and make a positive impact on communities in need.

She embraced change by viewing it as an opportunity for growth. When her hospital implemented a new electronic health record system, Sophia volunteered to be part of the implementation team. She saw this as a chance to learn new technology and contribute to the hospital's improvement efforts.

Networking and connecting with others were important to Sophia. She attended nursing conferences, joined professional organizations, and participated in local community events. These activities helped her build a network of supportive individuals who inspired and motivated her.

Sophia committed to lifelong learning by pursuing opportunities for education and self-improvement. She took online courses in leadership and management, attended workshops on patient care, and read books on personal development. Her curiosity and openness to new knowledge contributed to her continuous growth.

To cultivate resilience, Sophia built a strong support system of friends, family, and mentors. She practiced self-care by engaging in activities that nourished her body and mind, such as yoga, hiking, and spending time with loved ones. She developed healthy coping strategies, including mindfulness practices and journaling, to manage stress and adversity.

By maintaining a positive mindset, Sophia continued to practice positive thinking and reinforce her positive habits. She focused on her strengths, celebrated her achievements, and stayed optimistic about the future.

As a result of her continued transformation, Sophia experienced significant personal and professional growth. She advanced in her career, improved her health, and made meaningful contributions to her community. Sophia's journey demonstrates the importance of setting new goals, staying open to opportunities, and cultivating resilience to maintain a positive outlook on life.

Conclusion

MAINTAINING A POSITIVE outlook for life is an ongoing journey that requires continuous effort and commitment. By sustaining positive habits, reflecting on your journey, and looking forward with an open mind and resilient spirit, you can continue to transform your life and achieve greater success and fulfillment.

Sustaining positive habits involves incorporating practices such as gratitude, mindfulness, positive affirmations, physical activity, healthy eating, sleep hygiene, social connections, and continuous learning into your daily routine. These habits help to reinforce a positive mindset and contribute to overall well-being.

Reflecting on your journey provides valuable insights into your strengths, challenges, and areas for growth. Techniques such as journaling, meditation, self-assessment, vision boards, discussions with mentors, and gratitude practice help you stay connected to your goals and values, reinforcing your commitment to maintaining a positive outlook.

Looking forward, setting new goals, staying open to opportunities, and cultivating resilience are essential for continuous growth and transformation. Embrace a mindset of curiosity and exploration, be willing to take risks and try new things, and build a strong support system to navigate challenges and stay resilient.

By incorporating these practices into your life, you can unlock the potential for transformation and achieve greater success and fulfillment. Remember, the journey to maintaining a positive outlook for life is unique for each individual and requires ongoing effort and commitment. Embrace the process, be patient with yourself, and celebrate the positive changes that unfold. By nurturing a positive mindset, you can unlock the potential for a more meaningful and fulfilling life.

Conclusion

Recap of Key Concepts

AS WE REACH THE CONCLUSION of this book, it's valuable to take a moment to reflect on the key concepts we've explored and the principles that form the foundation of positive thinking. This recap serves as a summary of the essential ideas and strategies that can help you maintain a positive outlook and transform your life.

1. Understanding Positive Thinking: We began by defining positive thinking and exploring its significance. Positive thinking involves focusing on the good in any given situation, maintaining an optimistic attitude, and believing in one's abilities to overcome challenges and achieve goals. It is not about ignoring reality or avoiding difficult emotions but rather approaching life's difficulties with a proactive and hopeful mindset.

2. The Mind-Body Connection: We examined the profound impact that positive thinking has on physical health. Positive thoughts can enhance the immune system, reduce stress, and improve overall health outcomes. The mind-body connection highlights how our mental state can influence our physical well-being and vice versa.

3. Stress Reduction Techniques: Managing stress through positive thinking involves techniques such as mindfulness, meditation, deep breathing exercises, and physical activity. These practices help to calm the mind, reduce anxiety, and promote a sense of peace and well-being.

4. Healthy Lifestyle Choices: Adopting a healthy lifestyle, including balanced nutrition, regular exercise, and adequate sleep, supports a positive mindset. These habits contribute to physical health, which in turn fosters mental well-being.

5. Building Trust and Mutual Respect in Relationships: Positive thinking plays a crucial role in developing and maintaining healthy relationships. Trust,

mutual respect, effective communication, and conflict resolution are essential components that are enhanced by a positive outlook.

6. Effective Communication and Conflict Resolution: Positive communication involves active listening, empathy, and constructive feedback. It helps in resolving conflicts amicably and strengthens relationships by fostering understanding and cooperation.

7. Supporting and Encouraging Loved Ones: Offering support and encouragement with a positive mindset helps loved ones feel valued and empowered. It builds stronger emotional bonds and promotes a supportive environment.

8. Setting and Achieving Goals: Positive thinking is essential for setting realistic goals and achieving them. It involves believing in one's abilities, staying motivated, and maintaining focus on long-term objectives.

9. Embracing Change and Uncertainty: Change is a constant in life, and positive thinking helps in adapting to new circumstances with resilience and optimism. Embracing change involves viewing it as an opportunity for growth and staying open to new possibilities.

10. Lifelong Learning and Self-Improvement: A commitment to lifelong learning and self-improvement fosters personal growth and keeps the mind engaged. Positive thinking encourages curiosity, the pursuit of new skills, and continuous development.

11. Enhancing Productivity and Creativity: Positive thinking boosts productivity and creativity by fostering a solution-oriented mindset, reducing stress, and promoting a positive work environment. It encourages innovation and effective problem-solving.

12. Leadership and Positive Influence: Leaders who practice positive thinking inspire and motivate their teams, create a positive work culture, and drive organizational success. Positive leadership involves clear vision, resilience, and the ability to empower others.

13. Stories of Transformation: Inspirational case studies and personal anecdotes highlighted the transformative power of positive thinking. These stories demonstrated how individuals overcame adversity, achieved their goals, and found fulfillment through a positive mindset.

14. Maintaining a Positive Outlook for Life: Sustaining a positive outlook involves cultivating positive habits, reflecting on one's journey, setting new goals, staying open to opportunities, and building resilience. It is an ongoing practice that requires dedication and consistency.

Encouragement for the Future

AS YOU MOVE FORWARD in your journey, remember that maintaining a positive outlook is an ongoing process. It requires continuous effort, reflection, and adaptation. Life will inevitably present challenges, but with a positive mindset, you can navigate these difficulties with resilience and optimism.

1. Stay Committed to Your Positive Habits: The habits and practices you've learned are tools to help you maintain a positive outlook. Stay committed to them and incorporate them into your daily routine. Whether it's journaling, practicing gratitude, engaging in physical activity, or meditating, these habits will support your mental and physical well-being.

2. Embrace Lifelong Learning: Continue to seek out new knowledge and experiences. Lifelong learning keeps your mind active, fosters personal growth, and opens up new opportunities. Stay curious and open to the world around you.

3. Build and Nurture Relationships: Strong, supportive relationships are crucial for maintaining a positive outlook. Nurture your connections with family, friends, and colleagues. Offer support and encouragement, and don't hesitate to seek it when you need it.

4. Stay Resilient in the Face of Adversity: Challenges and setbacks are a natural part of life. When faced with difficulties, remember the resilience strategies you've learned. Stay focused on solutions, maintain hope, and view challenges as opportunities for growth.

5. Set New Goals and Pursue Your Dreams: Continue to set meaningful goals and pursue your dreams. Stay motivated and dedicated to your aspirations. Celebrate your achievements and use them as stepping stones to even greater success.

6. Reflect on Your Journey: Regularly take time to reflect on your journey. Assess your progress, celebrate your successes, and learn from your experiences. Reflection helps you stay connected to your goals and values and reinforces your commitment to maintaining a positive outlook.

Final Words of Inspiration

AS WE CONCLUDE THIS book, I want to leave you with a final message of inspiration. Positive thinking is a powerful force that can transform your life. It empowers you to overcome adversity, achieve your goals, and find fulfillment. By cultivating a positive mindset, you can unlock your potential and create a life filled with purpose, joy, and success.

Remember, the journey to maintaining a positive outlook is unique for each individual. It requires ongoing effort, patience, and commitment. Embrace the process, be kind to yourself, and celebrate the positive changes that unfold. With a positive mindset, you can navigate life's challenges with resilience and optimism, and achieve your dreams.

Stay positive, stay motivated, and continue to believe in yourself. The power of positive thinking is within you, and it has the potential to create a brighter future. Keep moving forward with hope and confidence, and remember that every step you take brings you closer to your goals and aspirations.

By incorporating the key concepts, habits, and strategies discussed throughout this book, you can maintain a positive outlook on life, achieve your goals, and create a fulfilling and successful future. Remember, the journey to positive thinking is ongoing, and with dedication and commitment, you can continue to grow, transform, and thrive.

Don't miss out!

Visit the website below and you can sign up to receive emails whenever Timothy Scott Phillips publishes a new book. There's no charge and no obligation.

https://books2read.com/r/B-A-KCQWC-JBGJF

BOOKS 2 READ

Connecting independent readers to independent writers.

About the Author

Timothy Scott Phillips is a dedicated author specializing in non-fiction self-help books that empower readers to overcome challenges and embrace personal growth. With a passion for mental health, resilience, and self-improvement, Timothy combines research-based insights with practical strategies to inspire lasting change. His work reflects a deep commitment to helping individuals navigate life's complexities, build confidence, and unlock their full potential. When he's not writing, Timothy enjoys mentoring, exploring nature, and connecting with his readers to share stories of transformation and hope. His books are a testament to the power of perseverance and the human spirit.

www.ingramcontent.com/pod-product-compliance
Lightning Source LLC
LaVergne TN
LVHW091048150826
845673LV00002B/502

* 9 7 9 8 2 2 7 7 4 1 8 1 3 *